A GRATEFUL HEART

A GRATEFUL HEART

365 Ways to Give Thanks at Mealtime

Edited by M.J. RYAN

Published by Mango Publishing, a division of Mango Media Inc.

Cover Design: Elina Díaz
Layout & Design: Claudia Smelser

 Originally published as Peaceful Kingdom in 1997 by Conari Press, ISBN: 1-57324-094-X.

For permission requests, please contact the publisher at:
Mango Publishing Group
5966 South Dixie Highway, Suite 300
Miami, FL 33143

For special orders, quantity sales, course adoptions and corporate sales, please email the publisher at sales@mango.bz. For trade and wholesale sales, please contact Ingram Publisher Services at customer.service@ingramcontent.com or +1.800.509.4887.

A Grateful Heart: 365 Ways to Give Thanks at Mealtime

Library of Congress Cataloging-in-Publication Data.
ISBN: (print) 978-1-6-8481779-5
BISAC: FAM002000, FAMILY & RELATIONSHIPS / Activities

Printed in the United States of America

To

Daphne Rose Kingma,
who taught me the profound effects
of saying thanks,
and to
Donald E. McIlraith,
whose embodiment of gratitude
is a daily inspiration,
I lovingly dedicate this book.

Contents

Introduction

In relation to others, gratitude is good manners;
in relation to ourselves, it is a habit
of the heart and a spiritual discipline.

—Daphne Rose Kingma

A couple of days before I was to write the introduction to this book, I was making dinner. Unexpectedly, the water main up the street broke and all water was cut off for several hours. Anyone who has tried to cook with no water knows how frustrating that experience can be. As I struggled along I suddenly realized what a lesson I was being given. Here I was, for the previous six months reading every known book (or at least it felt that way) that in any way related to giving thanks, and I had taken completely for granted the miracle of water coming out of my tap whenever I wanted it! If I could overlook that, what other blessings in my life had I not perceived?

Gratefulness—"great fullness," as Brother David Steindl-Rast reminds us, "is the full response of the human heart to the gratuitousness of all that is." Truly every single thing we *have* has been given to us, not necessarily because we deserved it, but gratuitously, for no known reason. And whatever source we believe is the giver—some concept of God or simply the breathtaking randomness of the universe—when we give thanks, we take our place in the great wheel of life, recognizing our connection to one another and to all of creation. Offering a blessing, reminds Brother Steindl-Rast, "plugs us into the aliveness of the whole world."

Howard Thurman once wrote, "To be alive is to participate responsibly in the experience of life," and for those of us who are uncomfortable within the structure of organized religion, finding a proper form for that responsibility has not been easy. We've tended to shy away from many of the rituals religion offers and too often have ended feeling disconnected and isolated. It is in the spirit of reconnection that this volume has been created.

That there is a deep hunger for connection—with ourselves, with one another, with nature, with the process of birth and death itself—is no surprise. What the writers here are offering, from a wide variety of spiritual disciplines and secular perspectives, is the awareness that setting aside time before we eat to acknowledge the blessings in our lives can go a long way to satisfy that hunger.

As I have spoken to people about this book, it is those with young children who've been the most excited. "So much of our time is consumed by the details of living; I want to find a way for my family to share the experience of being a part of something greater than just ourselves," said one mother. With that in mind, the book comprises 365 "blessings," both traditional and nontraditional, organized into four sections corresponding to the seasons, and designed to be used in a variety of ways. You may just open it and begin, reading one a day in the order given, using the ribbon to mark your place. Or you may pick and choose, using the index to find the topics you are interested in. Or you can open each evening at random and read what is offered.

I have tried to find selections on every possible human experience and could easily have filled volumes more. But I looked particularly for those that would speak to us all, regardless of spiritual orientation. Apropos of that, I have taken certain liberties with language, particularly patriarchal language (God almost always is male, particularly in those Christian prayers predating the late twentieth century). Bobby McFerrin's beautiful rendition of the Twenty-third Psalm on *Medicine Man* in which he changes all male pronouns to female is my inspiration for this.

I encourage you to try using *A Grateful Heart* every day as a ritual and see what happens as a consequence. "When was the last time, if ever, you saw anyone at McDonald's offer an expression of thanks (a prayer, a song, a dance) for his or her food?" asks Stephen Hyde in an article in *The Sun* entitled "Great Man Going." "Billions of burgers consumed yet not a solitary act of gratitude, individual or corporate, no festival to honor the bovine being in myth and art and imagination, or to celebrate the annual resurrection of the potato. How can this be? What kind of monstrous indifference to the taking of life does this suggest? What kind of heinous disrespect for the life that sustains human life? What is the real price we pay for the convenience of fast and plentiful food? Apathy, neglect, isolation? Or it is something deeper, the loss of relationship, of wholeness, of soul?...

"Once, the rituals of gratitude informed nearly every aspect of human life. Most of these we have abandoned or forgotten. Now, try to imagine this: for every one of those burgers sold, a song raised, a life recalled, a measure of grace restored."

—M. J. Ryan
Berkeley, California

Fall

Gratitude is heaven itself.

—William Blake

Thou that hast given so much to me,
Give one thing more, a grateful heart.
Not thankful when it pleaseth me,
As if thy blessings had spare days;
But such a heart, whose pulse may be thy praise.

—George Herbert

Now may every living thing, young or old, weak or strong, living near or far, known or unknown, living or departed or yet unborn, may every living thing be full of bliss.

—The Buddha

How easily we can forget how precious life is! So long as we can remember, we've just been here, being alive. Unlike other things for which we have a comparison—black to white, day to night, good to bad—we are so immersed in life that we can see it only in the context of itself. We don't see life as compared to anything, to not-being, for example, to never having been born. Life just is.

But life itself is a gift. It's a compliment just being born: to feel, breathe, think, play, dance, sing, work, make love, for this particular lifetime. Today, let's give thanks for life. For life itself! For simply being born!

—Daphne Rose Kingma

My whole being pulsates
with the fire of desire
for our everlasting union.
My very breath is but Yours.
My heart is a limitless beacon
of Your Love.

My Spirit, being Yours,
is the light of the world.
My eyes but radiate and reflect
our Perfect Love.
My very essence vibrates with You
as the harmony of music
not yet heard.

My vision is but Your Love
flowing through me,
seeing only its own reflection.
My only fulfillment is following Your
Directions and Guidance.

My voice, being Yours,
can only bless.
My prayer is but an eternal song of gratitude,

That You are in me,
and I am in You,
And that I live in Your Grace
forever.

—Gerald G. Jampolsky, M.D.

You who are smaller than the smallest seed; more beautiful than the rarest gem; Who hold the mountains and oceans in Your hand; Who breathes us with the breath of life; enfold us in Your great love that we may open our hearts to all mankind.

—Annabelle Woodard

Great Spirit, who hast blessed the earth that it should be fruitful and bring forth whatsoever is needful for the life of man, and hast commanded us to work with quietness, and eat our own bread; Bless the labors of those who till the fields and grant such seasonable weather that we may gather in the fruits of the earth.

—Adapted from *The Book of Common Prayer*

Today, today, today. Bless us...
and help us to grow.

—from the Rosh Hashanah liturgy

The Inner Light is beyond both praise and
blame,Like unto space it knows no boundaries;
Yet it is right here with us,
ever retaining its serenity and fullness.
It is only when you seek it that you lose it.
You cannot take hold of it nor can you get rid of it;
While you can do neither, it goes on its own way.
You remain silent and it speaks;
you speak and it is silent.
The Gate of Heaven is wide open
with not a single obstruction before it.

—YUNG CHIA

We join with the earth and with each other

To bring new life to the land
To restore the waters
To refresh the air

We join with the earth and with each other

To renew the forests
To care for the plants
To protect the creatures

We join with the earth and with each other

To celebrate the seas
To rejoice in the sunlight
To sing the song of the stars

We join with the earth and with each other

To recreate the human community
To promote justice and peace
To remember our children

We join with the earth and with each other

We join together as many and diverse expressions of one loving memory: for the healing of the earth and the renewal of all life.

—U.N. Environmental Sabbath Program

A bright autumn moon...
In the shadow of
each grass
an insect chirping

—Buson

The Lord is my shepherd, I shall not want. She maketh me to lie down in green pastures. She leadeth me beside the still waters. She restoreth my soul. She leadeth me in the paths of righteousness for her name's sake. Yea, though I walk through the valley of the shadow of death, I will fear no evil; for thou art with me; thy rod and thy staff, they comfort me. Thou preparest a table before me in the presence of mine enemies; thou anointest my head with oil; my cup runneth over. Surely goodness and mercy shall follow me all the days of my life; and I will dwell in the house of the Lord forever.

—Psalm 23:1, adapted

May the blessing of light be on you, light without and light within. May the blessed su nshine shine on you and warm your heart till it glows like a great peat fire, so that the stranger may come and warm himself at it, and also a friend.

—Traditional Irish blessing

When grapes turn
to wi ne, they long for our ability to change.

When stars wheel
around the North Pole,
they are longing for our growing consciousness.

Wine got drunk with us,
not the other way.
The body developed out of us, not we from it.

We are bees,
and our body is a honeycomb.
We made
the body, cell by cell we made it.

—Rumi, translated by Robert Bly

Blessed be you, harsh matter, barren soil, stubborn rock: you who yield only to violence, you who force us to work if we would eat. Blessed be you, perilous matter, violent sea, untameable passion: you who unless we fetter you will devour us. Blessed be you, mighty matter, irresistible march of evolution, reality ever new-born; you who, by constantly shattering our mental categories, force us to go ever further and further in our pursuit of the truth. Blessed be you, universal matter, unmeasurable time, boundless ether, triple abyss of stars and atoms and generations: you who by overflowing and dissolving our narrow standards of measurement reveal to us the dimensions of God...

—Teilhard de Chardin

I salute the breath of life in thee, the same life that is breathed by me, warm flesh to warm flesh, oily press of nose to nose, the hardness of foreheads meeting.
I salute that which gives us life.

—Keri Hulme

How do geese know when to fly to the sun? Who tells them the seasons? How do we, humans, know when it is time to move on? As with the migrant birds, so surely with us, there is a voice within, if only we would listen to it, that tells us so certainly when to go forth into the unknown.

—Elisabeth Kübler-Ross

O Great Spirit,
Whose voice I hear in the winds,
And whose breath gives life to all the world,
hear me! I am small and weak, I need your
strength and wisdom.

Let Me Walk In Beauty, and make my eyes
ever behold the red and purple sunset.

Make My Hands respect the things you have
made and my ears sharp to hear your voice.

Make Me Wise so that I may understand the
things you have taught my people.

Let Me Learn the lessons you have hidden
in every leaf and rock.

I Seek Strength, not to be greater than my
brother, but to fight my greatest enemy—myself.

Make Me Always Ready to come to you with
clean hands and straight eyes.

So When Life Fades, as the fading sunset,
my spirit may come to you without shame.

—Native American prayer

Help us, O Lord, to remember our kindred beyond the sea—all those who bend in bonds, of our own blood and of human kind—the lowly and the wretched, the ignorant and the weak. We are one world ... and one great human problem and what we do here goes to solve not only our petty troubles alone but the difficulties and desires of millions unborn and unknown. Let us then realize our responsibilities and gain strength to bear them worthily.

—W. E. B. Du Bois

Let us bless and let us extol, let us tell aloud and let us raise aloft, let us set on high and let us honor, let us exalt and let us praise the Holy One—blessed be He!—though He is far beyond any blessing or song, any honor or any consolation that can be spoken of in this world.

—The Kaddish

O beloved Pan, and all the other deities of this place, grant that I may become beautiful in my soul within, and that all my external possessions may be in harmony with my inner self. May I consider the wise to be rich, and may I have such riches as only a person of self-restraint can bear or endure.

—adapted from a speech by Plato

Grandfather,
Look at our brokenness.

We know that in all creation
Only the human family
Has strayed from the Sacred Way.

We know that we are the ones
who are divided
And we are the ones
Who must come back together
To walk in the Sacred Way.

Grandfather,
Sacred One,
Teach us love, compassion, and honor
That we may heal the earth
And heal each other.

—Ojibway people of Canada

We pray for the power to be gentle; the strength to be forgiving; the patience to be understanding; and the endurance to accept the consequences to holding to what we believe to be right.

May we put our trust in the power of good to overcome evil and the power of love to overcome hatred. We pray for the vision to see and the faith to believe in a world emancipated from violence, a new world where fear shall no longer lead men to commit injustice, nor selfishness make them bring suffering to others.

Help us to devote our whole life and thought and energy to the task of making peace, praying always for the inspiration and the power to fulfill the destiny for which we were created.

—ADAPTED PRAYER FROM WEEK OF
PRAYER FOR WORLD PEACE, 1978

Holy Spirit,
giving life to all life,
moving all creatures,
root of all things,
washing them clean,
wiping out their mistakes,
healing their wounds,
you are our true life,
luminous, wonderful,
awakening the heart
from its ancient sleep.

—Hildegard of Bingen, translated by Stephen Mitchell

All Life Is One
And Everything that Lives Is Holy
Plants, Animals and People.
All must eat to live and nourish one another
We bless the lives that have died to give us
this food.
Let us eat together
Resolving by our work to pay the debt of
our existence.

—JOHN BENNETT

May suffering ones be suffering free
And the fear struck fearless be.
May the grieving shed all grief—
And the sick find health relief.

—ZEN CHANT

We are all partakers of the bread of life,
Out of the lap of Mother Earth,
And from the hands of our human benefactors;
Many a life has been given for us,
Many a body has been broken for us,

We are all partakers of the water of life,
Out of the springs and streams of the earth,
And of the blood of life,
In uncounted sacrifices made in our behalf.

In ministrations such as these
    hath God nourished us;
Freely we have received, freely let us give.

—Robert French Leavens

Praise wet snow
    falling early.
Praise the shadow
    my neighbor's chimney casts on the tile roof
even this gray October day that should, they say,
have been golden.
Praise
the invisible sun burning beyond
    the white cold sky, giving us
light and the chimney's shadow.
Praise
god or the gods, the unknown,
that which imagined us, which stays
our hand,
our murderous hand,
    and gives us
still,
in the shadow of death,
    our daily life,
    and the dream still
of goodwill, of peace on earth.
Praise
flow and change, night and
the pulse of day.

—Denise Levertov

Lord of the World, I stand before you and before my neighbors—pardoning, forgiving, struggling to be open to all who have hurt and angered me. Be this hurt of body or soul, of honor or property, whether they were forced to hurt me or did so willingly, whether by accident or intent, whether by word or deed—I forgive them because we are human...I am ready to take upon myself the commandment, Love your neighbor as yourself.

—Levi Yitchak of Beditsche

Creator of the Stars
God of Epiphanies
You are the Great Star
You have marked my path with light
You have filled my sky with stars
    naming each star
    guiding it
    until it shines into my heart
    awakening me to deeper seeing
    new revelations
    and brighter epiphanies.

O Infinite Star Giver
I now ask for wisdom and courage
    to follow these stars
    for their names are many
    and my heart is fearful.

They shine on me wherever I go:
    The Star of Hope
    The Star of Mercy and Compassion
    The Star of Justice and Peace
    The Star of Tenderness and Love
    The Star of Suffering

The Star of Joy
And every time I feel the shine

I am called
to follow it
to sing it
to live it...

—MACRINA WIEDERKEHR

Do all the good you can
By all the means you can
In all the ways you can
In all the places you can
To all the people you can
As long as ever you can.

—JOHN WESLEY

Do not think that love, in order to be genuine, has to be extraordinary. What we need is to love without getting tired.

How does a lamp burn? Through the continuous input of small drops of oil. If the drops of oil run out, the light of the lamp will cease, and the bridegroom will say, “I do not know you” (Matthew 25:12).

My daughters, what are these drops of oil in our lamps? They are the small things of daily life: faithfulness, punctuality, small words of kindness, a thought for others, our way of being silent, of looking, of speaking, and of acting. These are the true drops of love . . .

Be faithful in small things because it is in them that your strength lies.

—Mother Teresa

May our hearts be pure, harmonious and peaceful.
May our Great Truth flourish and our worldly work
be prosperous and not offended by evil.
May all auspicious blessings be conferred.
May the benefits of yin and yang abundantly
aid our being and may we always be sheltered
by Heaven.

—FROM *WORKBOOK FOR SPIRITUAL DEVELOPMENT OF ALL PEOPLE*, P. 180

"Within each individual on this large and complicated world there lives an astonishing potential of greatness. Yet it is rare that these hidden gifts are brought to life unless by chance of fate," writes Velma Wallis. Acknowledging the truth of this statement, we take the opportunity right now to ask ourselves what unrevealed gifts we have to offer the world. What in us is being called for? What can we give that we haven't been giving?

Learn to turn to each person as the most sacred person on Earth, to each moment as the most sacred moment that has ever been given to us. This moment may never happen again, because no two moments are ever alike. Are we perhaps awake a bit more, perhaps breathing together with God?

—Reshad Feild

Matthew Fox once wrote, "The only hope Mother Earth has for survival is our recovering creativity—which is of course, our divine power. Creativity is so satisfying, so important, not because it produces something but because the process is cosmological. There's joy and delight in giving birth." Tonight we ask that each of us strive to tap into the creativity that is uniquely ours to give, and that we do so with a full measure of delight.

May we walk with grace
and may the light of the universe
shine upon our path.

—Anonymous

You never enjoy the world aright till the sea itself flows in your veins, till you are clothed with the heavens, and crowned with the stars; and perceive yourself to be the sole heir of the whole world; and more than so, because men are in it who are every one sole heirs, as well as you...

Till your spirit fills the whole world, and the stars are your jewels; till you are as familiar with the ways of God in all ages as with your walk and table; till you are intimately acquainted with that shady nothing out of which the world was made; till you love men so as to desire their happiness, with a thirst equal to the zeal of your own; till you delight in God for being good to all: you never enjoy the world...

You never enjoy the world aright till you see all things in it so perfectly yours that you cannot desire them any other way; and till you are convinced that all things serve you best in their proper places.

—Thomas Traherne

We are aware that all generations of our ancestors and all future generations are present in us.

We are aware of the expectations that our ancestors, our children, and their children have of us.

We are aware that our joy, peace, freedom, and harmony are the joy, peace, freedom, and harmony of our ancestors, our children, and their children.

We are aware that understanding is the very foundation of love.

We are aware that blaming and arguing never help us and only create a wider gap between us, that only understanding, trust, and love can help us change and grow.

—THICH NHAT HANH

True greatness lies not always
In the winning of worldly fame,
Nor doing our best spurred on by the cheers
And plaudits that follow our name.
But he who can face with a cheery grace
The everyday of life,
With its petty things that rasp and sting,
Is a hero in the strife.

—FANNIE HERRON WINGATE

The food is brahma (creative energy)
Its essence is vishnu (preservative energy)
The eater is shiva (destructive energy)
No sickness due to food can come
To one who eats with this knowledge.

—SANSKRIT BLESSING, TRANSLATED BY
BABA HARI DASS

Hear a prayer for courage.
Lord of the peaks,
Reared amid the thunders;
Keeper of the headlands
Holding up the harvest,
Keeper of the strong rocks.

—PRAYER TO THE MOUNTAIN SPIRIT

May the Ocean of Salt, the Ocean of Honey, the Ocean of Wine, the Ocean of Ghee, the Ocean of Curd, the Ocean of Milk, the Ocean of Sweet Water sprinkle thee with their consecrated waters.

—*MAHANIRVANA TANTRA X*

Thou Infinite One, it is Thy grace,
the highest opportunity for humanity
that we can sit and think and be together
to praise thee, O Lord.
O creative consciousness, O cosmos, moment of
positive existence, positive relationship,
positive love and brotherhood,
dedicated unto this, the highest reward on this
planet for the individual being,
and You are the one who granted it.
Our gratitude for this,
and may your blessings shower upon us
to make us healthy, happy, and holy
and may we live in a raised consciousness of
universal consciousness of love, peace,
and harmony.
Give us the power to exalt thee.
Give us the power to be thy channel.

—Yogi Bhajan

I arise each day
Through the strength of heaven:
Light of sun,
Radiance of moon,
Splendor of fire,
Speed of lightening,
Swiftness of wind,
Depth of sea,
Stability of earth,
Firmness of rock.

—ADAPTED FROM AN EARLY IRISH SONG,
ATTRIBUTED TO SAINT PATRICK

How would it be
if just for today
we thought less about contests and rivalries,
profits and politics,
winners and sinners,
and more about
helping and giving,
mending and blending,
reaching out
and pitching in?

How would it be?

—Anonymous

The birds have vanished into the sky,
and now the last cloud drains away.

We sit together, the mountain and me,
Until only the mountain remains.

—Li Po

Hail, hail, hail
May happiness come.
May meat come,
May corn come.
Just as the farmers work
And look forward to the reaping,
So may we sit again as we are sitting now.

—PRAYER OF THE NEW YEAR
FESTIVAL, THE GA OF GHANA

Let us all resolve: First to attain the grace of silence; Second to deem all fault-finding that does no good a sin ... Third to practice the grace and virtue of praise.

—HARRIET BEECHER STOWE

One does not need to fast for days and meditate for hours at a time to experience the sense of sublime mystery which constantly envelops us. All one need do is notice intelligently, if even for a brief moment, a blossoming tree, a forest flooded with autumn colors, an infant smiling.

—Simon Greenberg

I have a dream today.

I have a dream that one day every valley shall be exalted, every hill and mountain shall be made low, the rough places will be made plain,
and the crooked places shall be made straight,
and the glory of the Lord shall be revealed, and all flesh shall see it together.

—Martin Luther King, Jr.

I want to be your friend
For ever and ever without break or decay.
When the hills are all flat
And the rivers are all dry,
When it lightens and thunders in winter,
When it rains and snows in summer,
When Heaven and Earth mingle—
Not till then will I part from you.

—First-century Chinese oath of friendship

Attend me, hold me in your muscular flowering arms, protect me from throwing any part of myself away.

—Audre Lorde

Be at peace with your own soul, then heaven and earth will be at peace with you. Enter eagerly into the treasure house that is within you, you will see the things that are in heaven; for there is but one single entry to them both. The ladder that leads to the Kingdom is hidden within your soul ... Dive into yourself, and in your soul you will discover the stairs by which to ascend.

—SAINT ISACC OF NINEVEH

With grateful hearts the past we own;
The future, all to us unknown,
We to Thy guardian care commit,
And peaceful leave before Thy feet.

—PHILIP DODDRIDGE

Am I acting in simplicity, from a germ of the Divine life within, or am I shaping my path to obtain some immediate result of expediency? Am I endeavoring to compass effects, amidst a tangled web of foreign influences I cannot calculate; or am I seeking simply to do what is right, and leaving the consequences to the good providence of God?

—M. A. SCHIMMELPENNINCK

Not for the mighty world, O Lord, tonight,
nations and kingdoms in their fearful might—
Let me be glad the kettle gently sings,
let me be glad for little things.

—EDNA JAQUESTHE SUN BRINGS FORTH THE BEGINNING

The moon holds it in darkness
As above, so below
For there is no greater magic in all the world
than that of people joined together in love.

—WICCAN BLESSING

To be said looking at your hand:

Whose hand is this
that has never died?
Who is it who was born in the past?
Who is it who will die in the future?

If you look deeply into the palm of your hand, you will see your parents and all generations of your ancestors. All of them are alive in this moment ... Previous generations, all the way back to single-celled beings, are present in your hand at this moment.

—THICH NHAT HANH

I have perceiv'd that to be with
those I like is enough,
To stop in company with the rest
at evening is enough,
To be surrounded by beautiful, curious, breathing,
laughing flesh is enough.

—Walt Whitman, "I Sing The Body Electric"

You spent the first half of your life becoming somebody. Now you can work on becoming nobody, which is really somebody. For when you become nobody there is no tension, no pretense, no one trying to be anyone or anything. The natural state of the mind shines through unobstructed—and the natural state of the mind is pure love.

—Ram Dass

Thankful may I ever be for everything that
God bestows.
Thankful for the joys and sorrows, for the blessings
and the blows.
Thankful for the wisdom gained through
hardships and adversity.
Thankful for the undertones as well as for
the melody.

Thankful may I ever be for benefits both
great and small—
and never fail in gratitude for that divinest gift
of all:
the love of friends that I have known in times of
failures and success.
O may the first prayer of the day be always one of
thankfulness.

—Patience Strong

Oh, come to the water all you who are thirsty;
though you have no money, come!
Buy corn without money, and eat,
and, at no cost, wine and milk.
Why spend money on what is not bread,
your wages on what fails to satisfy?
Listen, listen to me, and you will have good things
to eat and rich food to enjoy.
Pay attention, come to me;
listen, and your soul will live.

—Isaiah 55:1-11

Inasmuch as the great Father has given us this year an abundant harvest of Indian corn, wheat, beans, squashes, and garden vegetables, and has made the forests to abound with game and the sea with fish and clams, and inasmuch as He ... has spared us from pestilence and disease, has granted us freedom to worship God according to the dictates of our own conscience; now, I, your magistrate, do proclaim that all ye Pilgrims, with your wives and little ones, do gather at ye meeting house, on ye hill, between the hours of 9 and 12 in the day time, on Thursday, November 29th of the year of our Lord one thousand six hundred and twenty-three, and the third year since ye Pilgrims landed on ye Pilgrim Rock, there to listen to ye pastor, and render thanksgiving to ye Almighty God for all His blessings.

—William Bradford, governor of Plymouth Colony, Thanksgiving proclamation, 1623

Give us thankful hearts ... in this the season of Thy Thanksgiving. May we be thankful for health and strength, for sun and rain and peace. Let us seize the day and the opportunity and strive for that greatness of spirit that measures life not by its disappointments but by its possibilities, and let us ever remember that true gratitude and appreciation shows itself neither in independence nor satisfaction but passes the gift joyfully on in larger and better form.

—W. E. B. Du Bois

Come, ye thankful people, come.
Raise the song of harvest home;
All is safely gathered in,
Ere the winter storms begin.

—Henry Alford

The reality that is present to us and in us:
call it Being ... Silence.
And the simple fact that by being attentive,
by learning to listen
(or recovering the natural capacity to listen)
we can find ourself engulfed in such happiness
that it cannot be explained:
the happiness of being at one with everything
in that hidden ground of Love
for which there can be no explanations....
May we all grow in grace and peace,
and not neglect the silence that is printed
in the centre of our being.
It will not fail us.

—THOMAS MERTON

Make a [silent] prayer acknowledging yourself as a vehicle of light, giving thanks for all that has come today.

—DHYANI YWAHOO

The great sea
Has sent me adrift
It moves me
As the weed in a great river
Earth and the great weather
Move me
Have carried me away
And move my inward parts with joy.

—Uvavnuk, an Eskimo shaman woman

Bless these Thy gifts, most gracious God,
  From whom all goodness springs;
Make clean our hearts and feed our souls
  With good and joyful things.

—Traditional Christian grace

Love means to love that which is unlovable,
  or it is no virtue at all;
forgiving means to pardon the unpardonable,
  or it is no virtue at all;
faith means believing the unbelievable,
  or it is no virtue at all;
And to hope means hoping when things
are hopeless,
  or it is no virtue at all.

—G. K. Chesterton

With the first mouthful, I promise to practice
  loving kindness.
With the second, I promise to help relieve the
  suffering of others.
With the third, I promise to see others' joy
  as my own.
With the fourth, I promise to learn the way of non-
  attachment and equanimity.

—Thich Nhat Hanh

Most gracious Spirit, by whose knowledge the depths are broken up, and the clouds drop down the dew; we yield thee unfeigned thanks and praise for the return of seed-time and harvest, for the increase of the ground and the gathering in of the fruits thereof, and for all the other blessings bestowed upon us.

—Adapted from
The Book of Common Prayer

May all things move and be moved in me
    and know and be known in me
May all creation
    dance for joy within me

—Chinook PsalterFriend, is sugar
sweeter or He who makes the sugar?

Friend, is the moon fairer or He who makes the moon?

Forgo sugars, forgo moons; He knows something other, He makes something other.

In the sea are marvels besides pearls, but none like the Monarch who makes the sea and the pearls.

Beside the water is another water springing from a marvelous waterwheel; without flaw and unsleeping It provides sustenance to the heart.

—Rumi, translated by A. J. Arberry

I move through my day-to-day life with a sense of appreciation and gratitude that comes from knowing how fortunate I truly am and how unearned all that I am thankful for really is. To have this perspective in my everyday consciousness is in itself a gift, for it leads to feeling "graced," or blessed, each time.

—Jean Shinoda Bolen

Each day I learn more than I teach;
I learn that half knowledge of another's life
Leads to false judgment;
I learn that there is a surprising kinship
    In human nature;
I learn that it is a wise father who knows his son;
I learn that what we expect we get;
I learn that there's more good than evil
    in this world;
That age is a question of spirit;
That youth is the best of life
No matter how numerous its years;
I learn how much there is to learn.

—Virginia Church

Give all to love;
Obey thy heart;
Friends, kindred, days,
Estate, good fame,
Plans, credit and the Muse,
Nothing refuse.

'Tis a brave master;
Let it have scope:
Follow it utterly,
Hope beyond hope:
High and more high
It dives into noon,
With wing unspent,
Untold intent;
But it is a god,
Knows its own path,
And the outlets of the sky.

It was never for the mean;
It requireth courage stout,
Souls above doubt,
Valour unbending:
Such 'twill reward;

They shall return
More than they were,
and ever ascending...

—Ralph Waldo Emerson

I aint what I wana be
I aint what I'm gona be
but Oh Lord
I aint what I used to be.

—Author of *An Unknown Slave*

Touch the world from the place centered in the heart and remain the selfless bearer of truth.

Beckon not self-serving illusions to fill the void of time and space, but reach to the core to produce a reality of the one vision of hope.

Come to the world with an openness of heart and lay to rest the falsehood of desire, the fear of wanting, and the futility of pursuit.

Live in Spirit's Will and all will be fulfilled through the pure power of Creation. All will be, beyond your imaginings.

Claim the Light that is yours to bear and carry the lantern of love into the darkened world of illusions.

Perceive not Spirit's plan, but go into the joy of the now. All will come to pass in perfect harmony if you but believe it is so.

Go in the peace that the moment is now.
Go in love, for that is what you are.

—DIANE V. CIRINCIONE

El Shaddai [translated from the Hebrew as
breasted god],
You are the earth beneath our feet,
the ground of our being,
and the Womb of all.
You birth the earth,
groaning with great labor pain in all our suffering
and dying.
Your golden joys and scarlet sorrows
fall onto death's dark soil,
and nourish the grain that becomes the Bread
of Life.
We harvest Your bounty,
we feast on Your beauty,
and are nourished and comforted at the breasts of
Your goodness.

—ANONYMOUS TWENTIETH-CENTURY PRAYER

O Thou in whose great arms
All the children of earth are embraced,
Here in thy presence we remember
  our kinship with all human kind.

We rejoice for those who are in
  full health and strength,
Whose ways are ways of pleasantness
  and peace.

Our hearts reach out toward those
  whose ways are ways of suffering,
  of body, mind, or soul.

May it be that thou shalt find us
  reaching out to them
Not only with our hearts but with
  our hands also,
To help them in the bearing of
  their burdens,
To help in the lifting of their
  burdens.

—Robert French Leavens

May all beings have happiness and the causes of happiness;
    this is immeasurable loving kindness;
May all beings be liberated from suffering and the causes of suffering;
    this is immeasurable compassion;
May all beings be free of suffering and always stay happy;
    this is immeasurable joy;
May all beings be free of grasping and aversion towards others, and develop faith in the equality of all beings;
    this is immeasurable equanimity.

—THE FOUR IMMEASURABLE VOWS,
TANTRIC BUDDHISM

It is love that fashions us into the fullness of our being—not our looks, not our work, not our wants, not our achievements, not our parents, not our status, not our dreams. These all are the fodder and the filler, the navigating fuels of our lives; but it is love: who we love, how we love, why we love, and that we love which ultimately shapes us.

It is love, before all and after all, in the beginning and in the end, that creates us. Today, remembering this, let yourself acknowledge and remember the moments, events, and people who bring you, even momentarily, into a true experience of love, and allow the rest, the inescapable mundanities of life, like a cloud, to very quietly drift away.

—Daphne Rose Kingma

May beings all live happily and safe
And may their hearts rejoice within themselves.
Whatever there may be with breath of life,
Whether they be frail or very strong,
Without exception, be they long or short
Or middle-sized, or be they big or small,
Or thick, or visible, or invisible,
Or whether they dwell far or they dwell near,
Those that are here, those seeking to exist—
May beings all rejoice within themselves.
Let no one bring about another's ruin
And not despise in any way or place,
Let them not wish each other any ill
From provocation or from enmity.

—THE BUDDHA, SUTTA NIPATA

We watch the water falling.
It looks just like a man
At the moment he says
I do at a ceremony
That the water, still so long
Doesn't fully understand
Or agree with.

We see fire that is hungrier
Than any workman wanting
Dinner after a hard day's labor.
It gobbles up everything.
In both worlds and refuses
To go out no matter how much
Rain it receives.

Being told "Good morning, would
You like tea or coffee?"
By a friend that watches water,
Loves fire, and other sacred
Ordinary moments, and scenes
Is like a visit to the rim of a
Canyon. We're not exactly sure

Whether to jump, to fly or
To simply stare and weep.

—John Levy, "Watching Friendship"

Gratitude before me,
gratitude behind me,
gratitude to the left of me,
gratitude to the right of me,
gratitude above me,
gratitude below me,
gratitude within me,
gratitude all around me.

—Angeles Arrien

Who loves the rain,
  And loves his home,
And looks on life with quiet eyes,
  Him will I follow through the storm,
  And at his hearth-fire keep me warm;
Nor hell nor heaven shall that soul surprise
  Who loves the rain,
  And loves his home,
And looks on life with quiet eyes.

—Francis Shaw

O Hidden Life, vibrant in every atom,
O Hidden Light, shining in every creature,
O Hidden Love, embracing all in Oneness,
May we each who feels himself as one with Thee
Know he is therefore one with every other.

—Annie Besant

Father-Mother of the Universe, in the beauty of Your Presence we give thanks for family and friends and for the clan of man. Nourish our bodies with these gifts of the earth and our minds with the thoughts sparkling among us. We will that our personal will be in atonement with the Divine as our Spirits bow in awe and wonder of the Great Unseen.

—Annabelle Woodard

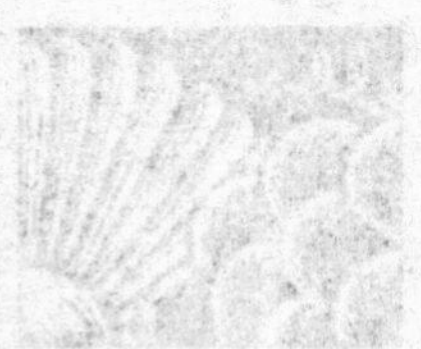

WINTER

A thankful person is thankful
under all circumstances.
A complaining soul complains even if
he lives in paradise.

—BAHA'U'LLAH

It is difficult to know what to do
    with so much happiness.
With sadness there is something to rub against,
a wound to tend with lotion and cloth.
When the world falls in around you, you have
pieces to pick up,
something to hold in your hands,
    like ticket stubs or change.

But happiness floats.
It doesn't need you to hold it down.
It doesn't need anything.
Happiness lands on the roof of the
    next house, singing,
and disappears when it wants to.
You are happy either way.
Even the fact that you once lived in
    a peaceful tree house
and now live over a quarry of noise and dust
cannot make you unhappy.
Everything has a life of its own,
it too could wake up filled with possibilities
of coffee cake and ripe peaches,

and love even the floor which needs to be swept,
the soiled linens and scratched records...

Since there is no place large enough
to contain so much happiness,
you shrug, you raise your hands,
and it flows out of you
into everything you touch. You are not responsible.
You take no credit, as the night sky takes no credit
for the moon, but continues to hold it,
and share it,
and in that way, be known.

—Naomi Shihab Nye,
"So Much Happiness"

When the song of the angels is stilled,
When the star in the sky is gone,
When the kings and princes are home,
When the shepherds are back with their flock,
The work of Christmas begins:
To find the lost,
To heal the broken,
To feed the hungry,
To release the prisoner,
To rebuild the nations,
To bring peace among brothers,
To make music in the heart.

—HOWARD THURMAN "THE WORK OF CHRISTMAS"

Round the table
Peace and joy prevail.
May all who share
this season's delight
enjoy countless more.

—CHINESE BLESSING

I will light candles this Christmas
Candles of joy, despite all sadness,
Candles of hope where despair keeps watch.
Candles of courage where fear is ever present,
Candles of peace for tempest-tossed days,
Candles of grace to ease heavy burdens.
Candles of love to inspire all my living,
Candles that will burn all the year long.

—Howard Thurman

I heard the bells on Christmas Day
Their old, familiar carols play,
And wild and sweet
The words repeat
Of peace on earth, good will to men!

—Henry Wadsworth Longfellow
"Christmas Bells"

Lord Jesus Christ, beloved Son, Wisdom, Word, and Light of Light from the all-merciful Abba, the Hidden Father. Cleanse me, a conditioned one, a sinner, enlighten and deify me, through the descent of the Holy Spirit, on behalf of all and as all in all. All-holy ever-virgin Mary, bride and mother of God, illumine this body, mind, will, heart, soul, spirit, the universe and all humanity.

—Lex Hixon, from the Christian tra

O Mother of the Universe, glorious in all your forms and as the formless clear light of nondual awareness! You alone are projecting various images of self and world for the evolution of consciousness, and you alone dissolve these images for the liberation of consciousness. You are mother and father, wife and husband, sister, brother, child, teacher, friend, and beloved. You are the single essence of all gods and goddesses, the single core of all religions. You are my True Self. You. You. Only You.

—Lex Hixon, from the Hindu tradition

Infinite mind-streams flowing throughout beginningless time have been my mothers and have thus poured forth inconceivable tenderness and loving sacrifice for me. To all these beloved, intimately connected living beings, who are manifesting as animals, humans, gods, and demons, I now offer profound gratitude. I vow to liberate all of them from their complex and painful emotional and conceptual bondage. I vow to struggle for their physical and spiritual well-being throughout all my future lifetimes. I vow to bring them all, through the powerful teaching of the Buddhas, into the Final Nirvana of nondual emptiness and bliss.

—Lex Hixon, from the Buddhist tradition

The primary spiritual weakness of human beings is their lack of constant, heartfelt gratitude directed toward the Source and Goal of the universe. The history of humanity testifies clearly to this fundamental thanklessness. Persons commit vast amounts of energy to acquiring and enjoying the abundant goods of earthly life, without making serious efforts to know and consciously praise the Source of Life.

At the end of time, those asleep in death will suddenly awaken, and the secrets of every heart and mind will shine forth, illuminated by the Source of Light who is intimately acquainted with all souls. On that infinite Day, humanity will recognize its own extreme ingratitude, and will humbly know true gratitude at last.

—HOLY QURAN 100:6-11
RENDERED BY LEX HIXON

Let us be still an instant and forget all things we ever learned, all thoughts we had and every preconception that we hold of what things mean and what their purpose is. Let us remember not our own ideas of what the world is for—we do not know. Let every image held of everyone be loosened from our minds and swept away.

—A Course in Miracles

Give Thy blessing, we pray Thee, to our daily work, that we may do it in faith, and heartily.

—Thomas Arnold

I remember with gratitude the fruits of the labors of others, which I have shared as a part of the normal experience of daily living.

I remember the beautiful things that I have seen, heard, and felt—some, as a result of definite seeking on my part, and many that came unheralded into my path, warming my heart and rejoicing my spirit.

I remember the moments of distress that proved to be groundless and those that taught me profoundly about the evilness of evil and the goodness of good.

I remember the new people I have met, from whom I have caught glimpses of the meaning of my own life and the true character of human dignity.

I remember the dreams that haunted me during the year, keeping me ever mindful of goals and hopes which I did not realize but from which I drew inspiration to sustain my life and keep steady my purposes.

I remember the awareness of the spirit of God that sought me out in my aloneness and gave to me a sense of assurance that undercut my despair and confirmed my life with new courage and abiding hope.

—HOWARD THURMAN,
"BLESSINGS AT YEAR END"

This plate is filled with food.
I am aware that each morsel is the fruit of much
hard work
By those who produced it.

—THICH NHAT HANH

We pray tonight, O God, for confidence in ourselves, our powers and our purposes in this beginning of a New Year. Ward us from all lack of faith and hesitancy and inspire in us not only the determination to do a year's work well, but the unfaltering belief that what we wish to do, we will do. Such Faith, O Lord, is born of Works. Every deed accomplished finishes not only itself but is fallow ground for future deeds. Abundantly endow us, Our Father, with this deed-born Faith.

—W. E. B. Du Bois

Drop Thy still dews of quietness,
Till all our strivings cease;
Take from our souls the strain and stress,
And let our ordered lives confess
The beauty of Thy peace.

—John Greenleaf Whittier
"Dear Lord and Father of Mankind"

Wild air, world-mothering air,
Nestling me everywhere,
That each eyelash or hair
Girdles, goes home betwixt
The fleeciest, frailest-flixed
Snowflake; that's fairly mixed
With riddles, and is rife
In every least thing's life;
This needful, never spent,
And nursing element;
My more than meat and drink,
My meal at every wink;
This air, which, by life's law,
My lung must draw and draw
Now but to breathe its praise.

—GERARD MANLEY HOPKINS

Food is not merely something we eat. It is a ceaseless reminder that we are mortal, earthbound, hungry, and in need. We are bound by a biological imperative that forever keeps us returning to the soil, plants, animals, and running waters for replenishment. Eating is life. Each time we eat, the soul continues its earthly journey. With every morsel of food swallowed a voice says, "I choose life. I choose to eat, for I yearn for something more."

—Marc David

May the passions of lust, anger, greed, pride and attachment depart from me. O Lord, I come to seek Thy shelter: Bless me with thy grace.

—Sacred song of the Sikhs

We thank you now for love, the great, the miraculous gift. For love in the body that comforts, for love in the emotional body that delights and frustrates and instructs, for the love of our sacred circle of friends, for love in the spirit beyond all walls and wounds, bounds and ends.

Love, we thank you for love, love that stirs and soothes us, love that gathers us into all joy and delivers us from all brokenness. Love that hears the soundless language, love that imagines and dreams, that can conquer all and willingly surrenders everything. Love that brought us into our lives and love that will carry us home.

—Daphne Rose Kingma

The creative energy of Heaven
is our paternal source.
The receptive energy of Earth
is our maternal source.
All people are the offspring
of the same universal Origin.
Within my own true nature
are the same virtues
as those of the inspired sages...
I have love for all people
who are in their "winter" years
and wish them to live enjoyably.
I treat all the young ones kindly
and help them to have a good life.
The sick and needy are also
my brothers and sisters,
so I protect and shelter
them under my wings.
I assist the talented
and do not waste my own talents...

By knowing the principles of change
and always doing my best,
I hope to be in harmony
with the enduring Will of the universe.

—From *Workbook for Spiritual Development of All People*, p. 161-162

I vow to practice mindful breathing and smiling, looking deeply into things.
I vow to understand living beings and their suffering, to cultivate compassion and loving kindness, and to practice joy and equanimity.

—Thich Nhat Hanh

By wishes alone you cannot a livelihood make.
Roll up your sleeves, send your bucket down
With those that others send.
Then behold!
At times, it will come up full,
Full to the brim;
At times, full with mud,
And perhaps a little water.

—Abd al-Aswad al-Duwali

Before me, may it be delightful.
Behind me, may it be delightful.
Around me, may it be delightful.
Below me, may it be delightful.
Above me, may it be delightful.
All, may it be delightful.

—Navajo prayer

Do not fear the truth,
hard as it may appear,
grievously as it may hurt,
it is still right
and you were born for it.
If you go out to meet
and love it,
let it exercise your mind,
it is your best friend
and closest sister.

—Dom Helder Camara
"The Desert is Fertile"

May I reach
That purest heaven, be to other souls
The cup of strength in some great agony,
Enkindle generous ardour, feed pure love,
Be the sweet presence of a good diffused,
And in diffusion ever more intense!
So shall I join the choir invisible
Whose music is the gladness of the world.

—George Eliot

Flow with whatever may happen and let your mind be free. Stay centered by accepting whatever you are doing. This is the ultimate.

—Chuang Tsu

Hold on to what is good
    even if it is a handful of earth.
Hold on to what you believe
    even if it is a tree which stands by itself.
Hold on to what you must do
    even if it is a long way from here.
Hold on to life
    even when it is easier letting go.
Hold on to my hand
    even when I have gone away from you.

—PUEBLO VERSE

Homage to the omniscient one
May all good fortune come about.

—*THE DHAMMAPADA*

Immortal Love,
    all human loves excelling,
    of all human loves the source,
How shall we thank thee
    for the bonds of affection
    with which we are made members
    one of another?
To those who gave us birth and have
    nurtured us,
To those who have been the guides
    of our childhood and youth,
To those who are our brothers and sisters,
To those whose lives are linked with ours
    in bonds of friendship
To these, to all others, dear to us,
    present or absent,
    near or far,
    companions invisible,
    a cloud of witnesses surrounding us,
We pay the tribute of our grateful love,
And because of their faith in us,
Here before thee we pledge anew
    our loyalty to them.

—Robert French Leavens

No longer forward nor behind
I look in hope or fear;
But, grateful, take the good I find,
The best of now and here.

—John Greenleaf Whittier

Teach me your mood, O patient stars!
Who climb each night the ancient sky,
Leaving on space no shade, no scars,
No trace of age, no fear to die.

—Ralph Waldo Emerson

Do not care
overly much for
wealth, or power, or fame,
Or one day you will meet someone
Who cares for none of these things,
And you realize
How poor you have become.

—Rudyard Kipling

O God who art Peace everlasting, whose chose reward is the gift of peace, and who has taught us that the peacemakers are Thy children, pour Thy sweet peace into our souls, that everything discordant may utterly vanish, and all that makes for peace be sweet for us forever.

—Galasian

In soft whisperings from the heart,
The child within offers you always
The thread of your truth.

May you cherish that child, trust
That voice and weave that thread
Richly into the fabric of your days.

—Anonymous

O giver of each perfect gift!
This day our daily bread supply:
While from the Spirit's tranquil depths
We drink unfailing draughts of joy.

—Lyra Catholica

Life is so generous a giver, but we, judging its gifts by their covering, cast them away as ugly or heavy, or hard. Remove the covering, and you will find beneath it a living splendor, woven of love, by wisdom, with power.

Welcome it, grasp it, and you touch the angel's hand that brings it to you. Everything we call a trial, a sorrow or a duty, believe me, that angel's hand is there; the gift is there,
and the wonder of an overshadowing presence.
Our joys too: be not content with them as joys.
They too conceal diviner gifts.

And so, at this time, I greet you.
Not quite as the world sends greetings, but with profound esteem and with the prayer that for you now and forever, the day breaks, and the shadows flee.

—Fra Giovanni, A.D. 1513

Now we will feel no rain
for each of us will be shelter for the other.
Now we will feel no cold
for each of us will be warmth for the other.
Now there is no more loneliness
for each of us will be companion to the other.
There is only one life before us
and our seasons will be long and good.

—ADAPTED FROM AN APACHE
WEDDING BLESSING

Praised be my Lord for our mother the earth, that which doth sustain us and keep us, and bringeth forth divers fruit, and flowers of many colours, and grass.

—SAINT FRANCIS OF ASSISI

Endurance, cleanliness,
strength, purity
Will keep our lives straight
Our actions only for a good
purpose.
Our words will be truth.
Only honesty shall come from
our interaction
With all things.

—From the Lakota Sioux Sweat Lodge ceremony

May the food we are eating make us aware of the interconnections between the universe and us, the earth and us, and all other living species and us. Because each bite contains in itself the life of the sun and the earth, may we see the meaning and value of life from these precious morsels of food.

—adapted from Thich Nhat Hanh

Do everything with a mind that lets go. Do not expect any praise or reward. If you let go a little, you will have a little peace. If you let go a lot, you will have a lot of peace. If you let go completely, you will know complete peace and freedom. Your struggles with the world will have come to an end.

—Achaan Chah

Don't think about the future.
Just be here now.
Don't think about the past.
Just be here now.

—Ram Dass

The food which we are about to eat

Is Earth, Water, and Sun, compounded through the alchemy of many plants.

Therefore Earth, Water and Sun will become part of us.

This food is also the fruit of the labor of many beings and creatures.

We are grateful for it.

May it give us strength, health, joy.

And may it increase our love.

—Unitarian grace

May it please the supreme and divine Goodness
to give us all abundant grace
ever to know its most holy will
and perfectly to fulfill it.

—Saint Ignatius of Loyola

Be patient toward all that is unsolved in your heart and try to love the questions themselves like locked rooms or books that are written in a foreign tongue. The point is to live everything. Live the questions now. Perhaps you will then gradually, without noticing it, live your way some distant day into the answers.

—Rainer Maria Rilke

To be said while holding hands:

May the love that is in my heart pass from my hand to yours.

Dearest Lord, teach me to be generous.
Teach me to serve Thee as Thou deservest;
To give and not count the cost;
To fight and not to heed the wounds;
To toil and not to seek reward,
Save that I know that
I do Thy will, O God.

—Saint Ignatius of Loyola

I've read all the books but one
Only remains sacred: this
Volume of wonders, open
Always before my eyes.

—Kathleen Raine

Mighty God, Father of all,
Compassionate God, Mother of all,
bless every person I have met,
every face I have seen,
every voice I have heard,
especially those most dear;
bless every city, town, and
street that I have known,
bless every sight I have seen,
every sound I have heard,
every object I have touched.
In some mysterious way these
have all fashioned my life;
all that I am,
I have received.
Great God, bless the world.

—John J. Morris, SJ

Innumerable labors brought us this food; we
should know how it comes to us.
Receiving this offering, we should conside
whether our virtue and practice deserves it.
Desiring the natural order of mind, we should be
free from greed, hate and delusion.
We eat to support life and to practice the way
of Buddha.
This food is for the Three Treasures, for our
teachers, family and all beings.
The first portion is to avoid all evil;
the second is to do all good;
the third is to save all beings.
Thus we eat this food and awaken with everyone.

—Mealtime chant at Zen centers

As plentiful as the grass that grows,
Or the sand on the shore,
Or the dew on the lea,
So the blessings of the King of Grace
On every soul that was, that is, or will be.

—TRADITIONAL IRISH BLESSING

The million little things that drop into your hands
The small opportunities each day brings
He leaves us free to use or abuse
And goes unchanging along His silent way.

—HELEN KELLER

Peace be with you, Life!
Peace be with you, Awakening!
Peace be with you, Revelation!

Peace be with you, oh Day, who
Engulfs the darkness of the earth
With thy brilliant light!

Peace be with you, oh Night,
Through whose darkness the lights
Of heaven sparkle!

Peace be with you, Seasons of the Year!
Peace be with you, Spring, who
Restores the earth to youth!
Peace be with you, Summer, who
Heralds the glory of the sun!
Peace be with you, Autumn, who
Gives with joy the fruits of
Labour and the harvest of toil!
Peace be with you, Winter, whose
Rage and tempest restore to
Nature her sleeping strength!

—Kahlil GibranS

Sweet is the smile of home: the mutual look
When hearts are of each other sure;
Sweet all the joys that crowd the household nook,
The haunts of all affections pure.

—John Keble

Praised are You, Adonai our God, Guide of the Universe, who creates innumerable living beings and their needs, for all the things You have created to sustain every living being.
Praised are You, the life of the Universe.

—A Jewish blessing

The Light shines and lives in all. May I never forget that the darkest of creatures is also of the Light...

Love breeds love and is born and nurtured from tolerance and acceptance. Let me lay down the anxieties and frustrations in this life to seek and foster love all the while remaining unattached to the act and its results...

Spirit, friend of my flight, help me to journey homeward in view of your message, "Love binds all wounds, softens all roads, and frees the soul to fly home in peace."

—DIANE V. CIRINCIONE

Let today embrace the past with remembrance and the future with longing.

—KAHLIL GIBRAN

I add my breath to your breath
that our days be long on the Earth,
that the days of our people may be long,
that we shall be as one person,
that we may finish our road together.

—Pueblo prayer

From joy I came.
For joy I live.
And in sacred joy
I shall melt again.

—Yogananda

To every thing there is a season, and a time to every purpose under the heaven:

A time to be born, and a time to die; a time to plant, and a time to pluck up that which is planted;

A time to kill, and a time to heal; a time to break down, and a time to build up;

A time to weep, and a time to laugh; a time to mourn, and a time to dance...

A time to rend, and a time to sew; a time to keep silence, and a time to speak;

A time to love, and a time to hate; a time of war, and a time of peace.

—Ecclesiastes 3:1-4, 7-8

Just as sunset is as beautiful as sunrise, all things are beautiful in their season. So tonight we give thanks for age, and pray that we may hold in honor all those who graciously come to the winter of life.

Normal day, let me be aware of the treasure you are. Let me learn from you, love you, bless you before you depart. Let me not pass by in quest of some rare and perfect tomorrow. Let me hold you while I may, for it may not always be so. One day I shall dig my nails into the earth, or bury my face in the pillow, or stretch myself taut, or raise my hands to the sky and want, more than all the world, your return.

—Mary Jean Iron

As the sun illuminates
the moon and the stars,
so let us illumine
one another.

—Anonymous

I am grateful for and bless the act of creation and all my loving creators. To be alive is the greatest gift one can receive. Life, with its mystery, joy, love, pain, difficulties and opportunities. I bless them all as I bless the wonder of our existence and I bless all who use the gift of life to increase the quantity of love and healing we all require to survive. Peace.

—BERNIE SIEGEL, M.D.

Eat your bread with joy, drink your wine with a merry heart.

—ECCLESIASTES 9:7

If I am not concerned for myself, who will be for me? But if I am only concerned for myself, what good am I? And if now is not the time to act, when will it be?

—Hillel

This ritual is One
The food is One
We who offer the food are One
The fire of hunger is also One
All action is One
We who understand this are One.

—Hindu blessing

Tonight we ask that we each find what we love to do in life so that, in the words of Joseph Campbell, "our life experiences on the purely physical plane will have resonances within our innermost being and reality, so that we feel the rapture of being alive."

Do you have the patience to wait
 till your mud settles and the water is clear?
Can you remain unmoving
 till the right action arises by itself?

—Tao Te Ching

It takes courage to ask a question and truly pay heed to the answer.... From the highest level to the most practical level, all real questions come about from the pain of separation, the separation from the answer.... We are merely instruments through which the question can be asked and through which the question can be answered.

—Reshad Feild

Blessed are we who can laugh
at ourselves
for we shall never cease
to be amused.

—Anonymous

The dictionary defines night in terms of day and day in terms of night. Can we find a way to talk about light and dark without talking about good and bad? To love both day and night? Can we hold the beauty of both in the same breath?

—Ruth Gendler

Come, come, whoever you are,
Wanderer, worshipper, lover of leaving—
  it doesn't matter,
Ours is not a caravan of despair.
Come, even if you have broken your vows a
  hundred times
Come, come again, come.

—Rumi

Ward off from us, disease and weakness.
By day and night, lovers of sweetness, guard us.

—Rig-Veda

Note: The "lovers of sweetness" are two Vedic gods, the Asvins, inseparable twins. They are fond of mead and soma, a plant-juice liquor.

Earth, ourselves,
breathe and awaken,
leaves are stirring,
all things moving,
new day coming,
life renewing.

—Pawnee prayer

Who knows what form the forward momentum of life will take in the time ahead or what use it will make of our anguished searching? The most any one of us can seem to do is to fashion something—an object or ourselves—and drop it into the confusion, make an offering of it, so to speak, to the life force.

—Ernest Becker

Live in the present,
Do all the things that need to be done.
Do all the good you can each day.
The future will unfold.

—Peace Pilgrim

As a child
I was told and believed
that there was a treasure
buried beneath every rainbow.

I believed it so much that
I have been unsuccessfully
chasing rainbows
most of my life.

I wonder why
no one ever told me
that the rainbow
and the treasure
were both
within me.

—GERALD G. JAMPOLSKY, M.D.

For each of us food is the source of sustenance, the basis of life; and when we offer this gift to one another, we are not only nourishing each other's bodies, we are feeding one another's spirits. So receive—and give—the food of your life as the powerful gift it is.

—Daphne Rose Kingma

Everyone has a spirit that can be refined, a body that can be trained in some manner, a suitable path to follow. You are here for no other purpose than to realize your inner divinity and manifest your innate enlightenment. Foster peace in your own life and apply the Art of Peace to all that you encounter.

—Morihei Ueshiba

May people be well, may they be well,
Male, female, male, female,
Goats, cattle, boys and girls;
May they multiply themselves.
Bad luck go away from us...

—AN ELDER OF THE KITHURI CLAN,
THE MERU OF KENYA

Let us live happily, though we call nothing our own. Let us be like God, feeding on love.

—DHAMMAPADA

Kali, be with us.
Violence, destruction, receive our homage.
Help us to bring darkness into the light,
To lift out the pain, the anger,
Where it can be seen for what it is—
The balance-wheel for our vulnerable, aching love.
Within the act of creation,
Crude power that forges a balance
Between hate and love.

Help us to be the always hopeful
Gardeners of the spirit
Who know that without darkness
Nothing comes to birth
As without light
Nothing flowers.

Bear the roots in mind,
You, the dark one, Kali,
Awesome power.

—May Sarton

To those of us whose lives have been hidden from society, from those we love, from ourselves, we join in solidarity.

To those of us who have resisted isolation and stood up to fear, we give heartfelt affirmation.

In honor of those of us who have courageously, joyfully, burst into the fullness of our identities, we offer gratitude and blessing.

—Molly Fumia

At the end of life, our questions are very simple: Did I live fully? Did I love well?

—Jack Kornfield

I vow to offer joy to one person in the morning
and to help to relieve the grief of one
person in the afternoon.
I vow to live simply and sanely, content with just a
few possessions,
and to keep my body healthy.
I vow to let go of all worries and anxiety
in order to be light and free.

—Thich Nhat Hanh

Give me a sense of humor,
Give me the grace to see a joke,
To get some pleasure out of life
And pass it on to other folk.

—Anonymous

Lord make me an instrument of Your peace.
where there is hatred, let me sow love;
where there is injury, pardon;
where there is doubt, faith;
where there is darkness, light;
and where there is sadness, joy.
O Divine Master, grant that I may not
so much seek to be consoled as to console;
to be understood as to understand;
to be loved as to love,
For it is in giving that we receive,
it is in pardoning that we are pardoned,
and it is in dying that we are born to
eternal life.

—Saint Francis of Assisi

In Man's Search for Meaning, Victor Frankl wrote "We need ... to stop asking about the meaning of life, and instead to think of ourselves as those who [are] being questioned by life—daily and hourly. Our answer must consist, not in talk and meditation, but in right action and in right conduct. Life ultimately means taking the responsibility to find the right answer to its problems and to fulfill the task which it constantly sets for each individual.

These tasks, and therefore the meaning of life, differs from [person to person,] and from moment to moment." In that spirit, let us take a moment to explore what that meaning is in our lives right now.

Spring

Before you taste anything, recite a blessing.

—Rabbi Akiva

Angeles Arrien writes, "The capacity to acknowledge others is directly equated with our ability to extend gratitude. Cross culturally there are four ways we acknowledge one another: Acknowledge-ment of skills, character qualities, appearance, and the impact that others make on us. The great healers of the world are gifted in their capacity to use the four acknowledgments in equal proportions. A daily practice of gratitude would be extending those four acknowledgments to ourselves, to our loved ones, toward our friends and colleagues." Let us take a few moments right now to make those acknowledgements to at least one other person.

An these dark waters
drawn up from
my frozen well . . .
Glittering of spring

—Ringai

Empower me
to be a bold participant,
rather than a timid saint in waiting,
in the difficult ordinariness of now;
to exercise the authority of honesty,
rather than to defer to power,
or deceive to get it;
to influence someone for justice,
rather than impress anyone for gain;
and, by grace, to find treasures
of joy, or friendship, of peace
hidden in the fields of the daily
you give me to plow.

—Ted Loder

This world is nothing more than
    Beauty's chance to show Herself.
And what are we?
Nothing more than Beauty's chance to see Herself.
For if Beauty were not seeking Herself
    we would not exist.

Every particle of creation
    sings its own song
    of what is, and what is not.
The wise hear what is;
The mad hear what is not.
And only a cracked mirror
    will show a difference.

All your knowledge
    leads you in the wrong direction;
All your worship
    only puts you to sleep.
Insipid is this world
    which only believes in what is seen;
Here, taste the wine from this Cup
    which cannot be seen.

The one who has adorned himself
    with the Creator's form
Is the only one fit to guard
    the purity
    of both worlds.

On account of those who repeat His Name,
This Earth has become a paradise,
    an honored place
    in the order of creation.
God's love is on this Earth,
And the heavens forever bend over to greet Her.

—Ghalib, translated by Jonathan Star

We pray for children
    who sneak popsicles before supper,
    who erase holes in math workbooks,
    who can never find their shoes.
And we pray for those
    who stare at photographers from behind
        barbed wire,
    who can't bound down the street in a new
        pair of sneakers,
    who never "counted potatoes,"
    who are born in places we wouldn't be
        caught dead,
    who never go to the circus,
    who live in an X-rated world.
We pray for children
    who bring us sticky kisses and fistfuls of
        dandelions,
    who hug us in a hurry and forget their
        lunch money.
And we pray for those
    who never get dessert,
    who have no safe blanket to drag behind them,
    who watch their parents watch them die,

who can't find any bread to steal,
who don't have any rooms to clean up,
whose pictures aren't on anybody's dresser,
whose monsters are real.
We pray for children
who spend all their allowance before Tuesday,
who throw tantrums in the grocery store
and pick at their food,
who like ghost stories,
who shove dirty clothes under the bed, and
never rinse out the tub,
who get visits from the tooth fairy,
who don't like to be kissed in front of the
carpool,
who squirm in church or temple and scream
in the phone,
whose tears we sometimes laugh at and
whose smiles can make us cry.
And we pray for those
whose nightmares come in the
daytime,
who will eat anything,
who have never seen a dentist,

who aren't spoiled by anybody,
who go to bed hungry and cry themselves
to sleep
who live and move, but have no being.
We pray for children who want to be carried
and for those who must,
for those we never give up on and for those
who don't get a second chance.
For those we smother...and for those who will grab
the hand of anybody kind enough to offer it.

—Ina J. Hughs

O Great Spirit, whose care reaches to the uttermost parts of the earth; we humbly beseech thee to behold and bless those whom we love, nowabsent from us, and defend them from all dangers of soul and body.

—Adapted from The Book of Common Prayer

One more day to serve.
One more hour to love.
One more minute to praise.
For this day I am grateful.
If I awaken to the morning sun,
I am grateful.

—Mary Lou Kownacki, OSB

We invoke your blessing on all the men and women who have toiled to build and warm our homes, to fashion our clothing, and to wrest from sea and land the food that nourishes us and our children.

We pray you that they may have health and joy, and hope and love, even as we desire for our loved ones.

Grant us wisdom to deal justly with every man and woman whom we face in the business of life.

May we not unknowingly inflict suffering through selfish indifference or the willful ignorance of a callous heart...

—Walter Rauschenbusch

It is the wind and the rain, O God, the cold and the storm that make this earth of Thine to blossom and bear its fruit. So in our lives it is storm and stress and hurt and suffering that make real men and women bring the world's work to its highest perfection. Let us learn then in these growing years to respect the harder sterner aspects of life together with its joy and laughter, and to weave them all into the great web which hangs holy to the Lord.

—W. E. B. Du Bois

Before me peaceful
Behind me peaceful
Under me peaceful
Over me peaceful
Around me peaceful

—Navajo prayer

Holy Creator,
thank you for artists:
visual, verbal,
musical, kinesthetic,
spiritual...
Within their creative process
may we recognize
the divine in all creation
and be moved to awe
and wonder and worship.

—Chris Glaser

Tonight, let us honor silence, "the perennial flow of language, interrupted by words," as Ramana Maharishi calls it. May we respect the need for silence in our lives.

The highest good is like water.
Water gives life to the ten thousand things and
does not strive.
It flows in places men reject and so is like
the Tao [way].

Thirty spokes share the wheel's hub;
It is the center hole that makes it useful.
Shape clay into a vessel;
It is the space within that makes it useful.
Cut doors and windows for a room;
It is the holes which make it useful.
Therefore benefit comes from what is there;
Usefulness from what is not there.

—TAO TE CHING, TRANSLATED BY
GIA-FU FENG AND JANE ENGLISH

With malice toward none, with charity for all, with firmness in the right, as God gives us to see the right, let us ... achieve and cherish a just and lasting peace among ourselves, and with all nations.

—Abraham Lincoln
Second Inaugural Address

O Spring, how we've missed you. Stir us from our slumber. Blow away the dark storms of winter with your gentle breezes so we can see again the mountains of challenge that inspire us to climb higher. They've been there all winter, but we've been inside. The promise of change is all around—may we greet the new beginning with renewed energy and vigor.

Earth, condolences,
Earth, condolences,
Earth and dust,
The dependable one,
I lean upon you.
Earth, when I am about to die,
I lean upon you.
Earth, while I am alive,
I depend upon you.
Earth, while I am alive,
I depend upon you.
Earth that receives dead bodies,
The Creator's drummer says:
From wherever he went,
He has roused himself,
He has roused himself.

—Ashanti drum poem

Love is light, the huge mysterious power that enlivens not only our spirits but all of creation around us. The light that falls into our lives because we love and are loved is the light that will truly illumine us forever. It is the star we follow to stumble on magic, the moonlight of incredible romance and unbelievable passion, the sunlight of healing and growing, of spiritual well-being.

It is the light that enters our eyes when we behold the ones we adore, the light we create with our words, with the radiance of our spirits, with the whole beauty of our lives. Love is the light in which we live and breathe and love and dream. Love is the light that will fall on us, now and forever.

—Daphne Rose Kingma

Let the beauty we love be what we do. There are a hundred ways to kneel and kiss the ground.

—Rumi

If you eat well, you must speak well.

—Yoruba proverb

The ancient Africans taught that if a person is good to you, you must forever speak good of them ... In order to keep the good flowing, you must speak of it ... Everything we receive in life is food for our growth. If we eat from the plate, we must give thanks. Remembering, without that food, at that time, we may have starved.

—Ivanla Vanzant

I am content to follow to its source
Every event in action or in thought;
Measure the lot; forgive myself the lot!
When such as I cast out remorse
So great a sweetness flows into the breast
We must laugh and we must sing,
We are blest by everything
Everything we look upon is blest.

—W. B. Yeats, from "A Dialogue of Self and Soul"

To be said one by one in a circle while holding hands:

Let peace extend from my hand to yours, [name].

—Adapted from A Course in Miracles

May there be peace in the higher regions; may there be peace in the firmament; may there be peace on earth. May the waters flow peacefully; may the herbs and plants grow peacefully; may all the divine powers bring unto us peace. The supreme Lord is peace. May we all be in peace, peace, and only peace; and may that peace come unto each of us.

Shanti (Peace) — Shanti — Shanti!—

—THE VEDAS, TRANSLATED BY RAIMUNDO PANNIKER

I thank You God for most this amazing
day:for the leaping greenly spirits of trees
and a blue true dream of sky;and for everything
which is natural which is infinite which is yes

—E.E. CUMMINGS

To be said while lighting candles:

We begin by honoring the Light.
We light these candles for our families, our
beloveds, our friends, for all our relations;
For those who are near and for those from whom
we feel an unwanted distance;
For the newborn, for the elderly, and for all the
wounded children.
May the candles inspire us to use our powers
to heal and not to harm, to help and not to
hinder, to bless and not to curse.
May their radiance pour out upon our hearts,
and spread light into the darkened corners of
our world.

—ADAPTED FROM A PASSOVER
HAGGADAH BY RACHEL ALTMAN
AND MARY JANE RYAN

May God, like a mother eagle, spread the wings of Her love and protection over us throughout this night, and forever. Amen.

—Marchiene Vroon Rienstra

The Tao that can be told is not the
eternal Tao;
The name that can be named is not the
eternal name.
The Nameless is the origin of Heaven
and Earth;
The Named is the mother of all things.

—Lao Tzu, translated by
Wing-Tsit Chan

Resurrection. The reversal of what was thought to be absolute. The turning of midnight into dawn, hatred into love, dying into living anew.

If we look more closely into life, we will find that resurrection is more than hope, it is our experience. The return to life from death is something we understand at our innermost depths, something we feel on the surface of our tender skin. We have come back to life, not only when we start to shake off a shroud of sorrow that has bound us, but when we begin to believe in all that is still, endlessly possible.

We give thanks for all those times we have arisen from the depths or simply taken a tiny step toward something new. May we be empowered by extraordinary second chances. And as we enter the world anew, let us turn the tides of despair into endless waves of hope.

—MOLLY FUMIA

Holy be the white head of a negro,
Sacred be the black flax of a black child.
Holy be the golden down
That will stream in the waves of the wind
And will thin like dispersing cloud.
Holy be the heads of Chinese hair,
Sea calm, sea impersonal
Deep flowering of the mellow and traditional.
Heads of people fair
Bright shimmering from the riches of their species:
Heads of Indians
With feeling of distance and space and dusk:
Heads of wheaten gold,
Heads of peoples dark
So strong, so original,
All of the earth and the sun.

—George Campbell, contemporary
Jamaican poet

I hear Great Grandmother singing,
singing as she always has and always will
for she is the sound of all that lives:
she is the breath of the Earth.
She is the weeping of sadness, sorrow,
betrayal, treachery.
She is the voice of hope, joy, justice,
thunder of the ocean morning
of the river silence
of the cave wisdom
of the other shore.
I hear Great Grandmother singing,
singing through me.

—From Jewels on a String

Fill my heart with Love,
that my every teardrop may become a star.

—Hazrat Inayat Khan

Remain faithful to the earth, my brothers and sisters, with the power of your virtue. Let your gift-giving love and your knowledge serve the meaning of the earth. Thus I beg and beseech you. Do not let them fly away from earthly things and beat with their wings against eternal walls. Alas, there has always been so much virtue that has flown away. Lead back to the earth the virtue that flew away ... back to the body, back to life, that it may give the earth a meaning...

Verily, the earth shall yet become a site of recovery. And even now a new fragrance surrounds it, bringing salvation—and a new hope.

—Friedrich Nietzsche

Let us give thanks
for the food we are about to eat.
May there be food for all,
abundant and healthful.
Let us have the wisdom to choose to eat only that
which enhances our precious energy
and sustains us through our labors and rest.

—Adapted from An Haggadah of Liberation

O God
help me
to believe
the truth about myself
no matter
how beautiful it is!

—Macrina Wiederkehr

May I become a medicine for the sick and their
physician, their support until sickness
come not again.
May I become an unfailing store for the wretched,
and be first to supply them with their needs.
My own self and my pleasures, my righteousness
past, present and future, may I sacrifice without
regard, in order to achieve the welfare of beings.

—Santideva

The temple bell
stops ringing
but the sound keeps
coming
out of the flowers

—Basho

Earth Water Air and Fire combined to
make this food.
Numberless beings gave their lives and labor that
we may eat.
May we be nourished that we may nourish life.

—Joan Halifax

Once the guest has eaten and drunk at your table, the guest becomes kin ... beggar or enemy, friend or chief, if they knock on your door, it will open; if they seek your shelter, it will be given, and if they ask for hospitality, give them your bread and wine ... for who knows when you may need the help of a fellow human?

—Keri Hulme

Sh Great Spirit of Surprise,
dazzle us with a day full of amazing embraces,
capricious, uncalculated caring,
great hearts, kind souls and doers of
good deeds.

—MOLLY FUMIA

It's a beautiful world to see,
Or it's dismal in every zone,
The thing it must be in its gloom or its gleam
Depends on yourself alone.

—ANONYMOUS

May your life be like a
wildflower,
growing freely in the
beauty
and joy of each day.

—Native American proverb

Live in simple faith...
Just as this
trusting cherry
flowers, fades, and falls

—Issa

"There is a vitality, a life force, an energy, a quickening that is translated through you into action and because there is only one of you in all time, this expression is unique. And if you block it, it will never exist through any other medium and be lost, the world will not have it." So said dancer Martha Graham. Tonight we pray that each of us find our unique life force and express it as fully as we possibly can.

Tis this one hour that God has given;
His Now we must obey;
And it will make our earth a heaven
To live today—today.

—Lydia Avery Coonley Ward

Saint Augustine once said, "Men go abroad to wonder at the height of mountains, at the huge waves of the sea, at the long courses of the rivers, at the vast compass of the ocean, at the circular motion of the stars, and they pass by themselves without wondering."

Tonight we acknowledge the wonder of our physical incarnation—that we are here, in these particular bodies, at this particular time, in these particular circumstances. May we never take for granted the gift of our individuality.

From the rain-god food arises;
From worship comes the rain.

—Bhagavad Gita, 3:14

Dear Mother,
Hear and bless
Thy beasts
And singing birds:
And guard with tenderness
Small things
That have no words.

—ADAPTED FROM A TRADITIONAL CHRISTIAN PRAYER

Breathing in, I know I am
breathing in.
Breathing out, I know I am
breathing out.

—THICH NHAT HANH

Nothing is so beautiful as Spring—
When weeds, in wheels, shoot long and
    lovely and lush;
Thrush's eggs look little low heavens, and thrush
Through the echoing timber does so
    rinse and wring
The ear, it strikes like lightning to hear him sing;
The glassy peartree leaves and blooms, they brush
The descending blue; that blue is all in a rush
With richness; the racing lambs too have
    fair their fling.

—Gerard Manley Hopkins

—a phantom, dew, a bubble,
A dream, a flash of lightning, and a cloud;
Thus we should look upon all that was made.

—The Buddha

Gandhi once said, "What I am concerned with is my readiness to obey the call of Truth, my God, from moment to moment, no matter how inconsistent it may appear. My commitment is to Truth, not to consistency." May we, like Gandhi, see our lives as a series of experiments with the truth and make every effort to align our choices with the deeper truths of the universe.

May we do what we can each day, as impeccably as possible and then be at peace, for the results are out of our hands.

Radiant Sister of the Day,
Awake! arise! and come away!
To the wild woods and the plains,
And the pools where winter rains
Image all their roof of leaves,
Where the pine its garland weaves
Of sapless green and ivy dun
Round stems that never kiss the sun;
Where the lawns and pastures be,
And the sandhills of the sea—
Where the melting hoar-frost wets
The daisy-star that never sets,
And wind-flowers, and violets,
Which yet join not scent to hue,
Crown the pale year weak and new;
When the night is left behind,
And the blue moon is over us,
And the multitudinous
Billows murmur at our feet,
Where the earth and ocean meet,
And all things seem only one
In the universal sun.

—Percy Bysshe Shelley
"To Jane: The Invitation"

Blessings of a kind heart upon you;
Blessings of the eyes of compassion upon you;
Blessings of giving to the earth upon you;
Blessings of the wisdom of the seasons upon you;
Blessings of breathing freely upon you;
Blessings of this moment upon you.

—JACK KORNFIELD

The fruit of silence is prayer,
The fruit of prayer is faith,
The fruit of faith is love and
The fruit of love is silence.

—MOTHER TERESA

I love all that thou lovest,
Spring of Delight!
The fresh Earth in new leaves dressed,
And the starry night;
Autumn evening, and the morn
When the golden mists are born.

I love the snow, and all the forms
Of the radiant frost;
I love waves, and winds, and storms,
Everything almost
Which is Nature's, and may be
Untainted by man's misery.

I love Love—though he has wings,
And like light can flee,
But above all other things,
Spirit, I love thee—
Thou art love and life! Oh, come,
Make once more my heart thy home.

—Percy Bysshe Shelley

The Male holds the power
and is the reservoir of the power
The female taps the power in him
    and channels it
Neither one can work without the other
One without the other is incomplete

—Traditional Pagan blessing

Give me everything mangled and bruised, and I will make a light of it to make you weep, and we will have rain and we will have begun again.

—Deena Metzger

Tonight we reflect on paradox:
Water wears away rock
Spirit overcomes force
The weak will undo the mighty.
May we learn to see things backwards, inside out,
and upside down.

—ADAPTED FROM THE TAO TE CHING

To see a World in a Grain of Sand
And a Heaven in a Wild Flower,
Hold Infinity in the palm of your hand
And Eternity in an hour.

—WILLIAM BLAKE

"Through the resource of power we are able to show up. Through the resource of love we are able to pay attention to what has heart and meaning. Through the resource of vision we are able to give voice to what we see. Through the resource of wisdom we are able to be open to all possibilities and unattached to outcome," notes Angeles Arrien. May we find the power, the love, the vision, and the wisdom we need in our lives.

Dewdrop, let me cleanse
in your brief
sweet waters...
These dark hands of life

—Basho

I wandered lonely as a cloud
That floats on high o'er vales and hills,
When all at once I saw a crowd,
A host, of golden daffodils;
Beside the lake, beneath the trees,
Fluttering and dancing in the breeze.

Continuous as the stars that shine
And twinkle on the milky way,
They stretched in never-ending line
Along the margin of a bay:
Ten thousand saw I at a glance,
Tossing their heads in sprightly dance.

The waves beside them danced; but they
Out-did the sparkling waves in glee:
A poet could not but be gay,
In such a jocund company:
I gazed—and gazed—but little thought
What wealth the show to me had brought:

For oft, when on my couch I lie
In vacant or in pensive mood,
They flash upon that inward eye
Which is the bliss of solitude;
And then my heart with pleasure fills,
And dances with the daffodils.

—William Wordsworth

In the name of Allah, Most Gracious,
Most Merciful.
Praise be to Allah, the Cherisher and Sustainer
of the worlds;
Most Gracious, Most Merciful;
Lord of the Day of Judgment.
Thee do we worship, and Thine aid we seek.

—Quran, 1:1-5

O Mother-Father God of light, in the cradle of whose radiance we shine, and in whose translucent essence we are all becoming luminous, divided by nothing, encompassing all things, we pray for a healing of every division that has bound us in this life, and in particular for a resolution of the conflicts that have separated men from women.

Grant women the feminine grace to welcome men with patience, understanding, and wisdom, into the sacred world of emotion. Give men the masculine strength to guide women into the world of power and expression with generosity, dignity, and integrity of action.

Bring us together. Erase our differences. Open our arms and our hearts and allow us to share the blessings of our gender, each with the other, so we may all be rich in love, and not impoverished through conflict. Allow us to bask in the light of our beautiful sameness and make our relationships blossom with the welcome that is a pure reflection of your love for every being.

—Daphne Rose Kingma

Ask, and it will be given to you: seek, and you will find; knock, and the door will be opened to you. For everyone who asks, receives; and he who seeks, finds; and to him who knocks, the door will be opened.

—MATTHEW 7:7-8

That is perfect. This is perfect.
Perfect comes from perfect.
Take perfect from perfect, the remainder is perfect.
May peace and peace and peace be everywhere.

—THE UPANISHADS

"It was only when I lay there on rotting prison straw that I sensed within myself the first stirring of good," says Alexander Solzhenitsyn. "Gradually, it was disclosed to me that the line separating good and evil passes, not through parties, states, nor between classes, nor between political parties, either, but right through all human hearts. So, bless you, prison, for having been in my life." With Solzhenitsyn as our inspiration, let us take a moment to find the gift of one difficult thing we have faced and give thanks for its teachings.

May the One who gives life to the living,
give you a long and stable life.

—Babylonian Talmud

Life has meaning only in the struggles.
Triumph or defeat is in the hands of the Gods.
So let us celebrate the struggles.

—SWAHILI WARRIOR SONG

Come come! Come out!
From bogs old frogs
command the dark
and look ... The stars!

—KIKAKU

Wheat and weeds:
  let them grow together.
Arabs and Jews in Palestine:
  let them grow together.
Greeks and Turks of the Balkans:
  let them grow together.
Catholics and Protestants of Northern Ireland:
  let them grow together.
Pros and Contras of Central America:
  let them grow together.
Documented and undocumented aliens:
  let them grow together.
Immigrants and Native Americans:
  let them grow together.
Blacks and Whites of South Africa:
  let them grow together.
Sikhs and Hindus of India:
  let them grow together.
Revolutionaries and reactionaries:
  let them grow together.
Russians and Americans:
  let them grow together.

Religious leaders who lay and lighten burdens:
let them grow together.
Disciples prone to boasts and betrayals:
let them grow together.
People who wound and heal:
let them grow together.
Rich and poor, humble and haughty:
let them grow together.
Those whose thinking is similar and contrary:
let them grow together.
Those whose feelings are transparent or concealed:
let them grow together.
Days of spareness and days of plenty:
let them grow together.
Winter, spring, summer, fall:
let them grow together.
All the seasons of one's life:
let them grow together.
Joys and sorrow, laughter, tears:
let them grow together.
Strength and weakness:
let them grow together.

Doubt and faith:
let them grow together.
Denial and commitment:
let them grow together.
Preoccupation and freedom:
let them grow together.
Virtue and vice:
let them grow together.
Contemplation and action:
let them grow together.
Giving and receiving:
let them grow together.
The helpful and helpless:
let them grow together.
Wisdom of the East and West:
let them grow together.
All contrarieties of the Lord:
let them grow together.

—MICHAEL MOYNAHAN, SJ

Arise my beloved, my fair one and come away
For lo, the winter is past.
Flowers appear on the earth.
The time of singing is here.
The song of the dove
Is heard in the land.

—SONG OF SOLOMON 2:10-12

Albert Einstein once said, "There are two ways to live your life. One is as though nothing is a miracle. The other is as though everything is a miracle." Today we celebrate the miracle.

We pray for those who dance with life
in the face of death.
For those whose unkind visitor
brought them great limitation,
for whom the plague is real.

For the child, the woman, the old man;
the banker, the teacher,
the prisoner, the priest.
For the artist, the musician, the player.
For the worker, the lover of imagination,
the dreamer of dreams.

For those who were told not to love,
and dared to love anyway.
For those who hid for a lifetime,
and those who bravely ventured out.

For those who die alone,
and those who leave surrounded by love.
For all the victims of that dark night,
that they may reach the dawn of victory.

To them, we bow inwardly.
They are with us, now and in memory,
and in the hope of the new day.

—MOLLY FUMIA

May the
longtime
sun shine upon you,
all love surround you,
and the sweet light within you
guide your way on.

—TRADITIONAL BLESSING

To our prayers, O Lord, we join our unfeigned thanks for all thy mercies; for our being, our reason, and all other endowments and faculties of soul and body; for our health, friends, food, and raiment, and all the other comforts and conveniences of life.

—Adapted from The Book of Common Prayer

May Peace be with you in heart and mind and body. May you experience Grace and Healing Love. May you be lifted as Life opens windows through which the Eternal sends Light.

—Annabelle Woodard

The sun is the light of our lives. It is the sustenance of life, the mirror of our joy, the source of the light that we are inhabited by.

When the sun is shining our spirits are lifted, exalted by seeing the light. When the sun hides its face, our hearts are exhausted. We need, we feed on the light.

Today, give thanks for the sun: the life, the joy, the power, the source, the eye of God beholding us, in whose light we shine.

—Daphne Rose Kingma

As our bodies are sustained with this food,
May our hearts be nourished with true friendship
and our souls fed with truth.

From that which we fear, O Lord, make us fearless.
O bounteous One, assist us with your aid.
    Drive far the malevolent, the foeman.
May the atmosphere we breathe
breathe fearlessness into us:
fearlessness on earth
and fearlessness in heaven!
May fearlessness guard us
behind and before!
May fearlessness surround us
above and below!
May we be without fear
of friend and foe!
May we be without fear
of the known and the unknown!
May we be without fear
by night and by day!
    Let all the world be my friend!

—The Vedas, translated by
Raimundo Panniker

There is a force within that gives you life—
    Seek that.
In your body there lies a priceless jewel—
    Seek that.
Oh, wandering Sufi.
    if you are in search of the greatest treasure,
    don't look outside,
Look within, and seek That.

—Rumi, translated by Jonathan Star

Let us go around the table now and each of us speak about one blessing we received and one blessing we gave today.

—INSPIRED BY BROTHER
DAVID STEINDL-RAST

I am a spirit unto the Lord my God, and unto
humanity a human being.
May my spirit and my soul be eternally aligned
unto the Lord God.
I call forth all that lies in my spirit,
As I avail myself unto the all that is, the Creator of
Life and Light,
To be unto me in the highest level of conduct,
That my life and my light reflect the spirit that I
am, for unto God I am.
I commit to a life of a higher order,
That I shall live by the law of my highest being,
Of love and compassion, of joy and beauty, of
reverence for all life.
So be it. Amen.

—Jacqueline T. Snyder (Eagle Speaks Woman), Founder of Sacred Life Association

Mother, Father, God,
For the sacred circle of family and friendship,
we thank you and ask that, with your guidance,
we may widen and deepen those circles by
touching others with love and understanding.
Blessings be.

—Sue Patton Thoele

From the many who are ONE,
To the ONE WHO IS many,
Hallowed be OUR NAME
Blessings be unto US.

—Kenneth R. Kurtz

In On Judaism Martin Buber wrote, "Youth is the time of total openness. With totally open senses, it absorbs the world's variegated abundance; with a totally open will, it gives itself to life's boundlessness. It has not yet sworn allegiance to any one truth for whose sake it would have to close its eyes to all other perspectives." Let us take time right now to find that young part of ourselves—open to life's possibilities and willing to explore all options. May we always honor and nurture youth's gifts.

Come, fill the Cup, and in the fire of Spring
Your Winter-garment of Repentance fling:
    The Bird of Time has but a little way
To flutter—and the Bird is on the Wing.

—Rubaiyat of Omar Khayyam

O my guardians, from remote antiquity,
Watch over our home
From top to bottom;
From one corner to the other;
From east to west;
From (the side facing) the upland to
(the side facing) the sea;
From the inside to the outside.
Watch over and protect it;
Ward off all that may trouble our life here.
'Amana - [the prayer] is freed.

—Hawaiian daily house prayer

We dedicate this meal to our hopes and dreams
for the future.
We dream of a world not threatened by
destruction.
We dream of a world in which all people are free to
be themselves.
We dream of a world at peace.

—Adapted from An Haggadah of Liberation

It is written that "Everywhere, hands lie open to catch us when we fall." Let us give thanks tonight for this invisible support.

From food all creatures are produced
And all creatures that dwell on earth
By food they live
And into food they finally pass.
Food is the chief among beings...
Verily he obtains all food
Who worships the Divine as food.

—IN THE TAITTIRIYA UPANISHAD

Marvelous Truth, confront us
at every turn
in every guise

—DENISE LEVERTOV

All living beings are struggling for life,
May they all have enough food today.

—THICH NHAT HANH

Some poor villages
lack fresh fish
or flowers...
All can share this moon

—SAIKAKU

Summer

It is gratefulness which makes the soul great.

—Abraham Joshua Heschel

All things in this creation exist within you, and all things in you exist in creation; there is no border between you and the closest things, and there is no distance between you and the farthest things, and all things, from the lowest to the loftiest, from the smallest to the greatest, are within you as equal things. In one atom are found all the elements of the earth; in one motion of the mind are found the motions of all the laws of existence; in one drop of water are found the secrets of all of the endless oceans; in one aspect of you are found all the aspects of *existence*... [Thus] "Your life has no end, and you shall live forevermore."

—Kahlil Gibran

May God, the Giver of all wisdom, beauty,
and well-being,
bless all who love Her with these gifts,
and grant that Her blessings may be
generously shared.

—Marchiene Vroon Rienstra

Don't go outside your house to see flowers.
My friend, don't bother with that excursion.
Inside your body there are flowers.
One flower has a thousand petals.
That will do for a place to sit.
Sitting there you will have a glimpse of beauty
inside the body and out of it,
before gardens and after gardens.

—KABIR, TRANSLATED BY ROBERT BLY

Now I pray that each and every being's true nature be revealed, that we each see clearly our inherent truth and find liberation from the shackles of suffering and difficulty imposed by the limitations of our mind.

—CHAGDUD TULKU

O the east, O the west,
O the north, O the south,
O above, O below, O the sun,
Recognize me the fisherman.
Look at the grumbling, at the fruitfulness
We are first; ours is last.
Give recognition to me O the sun, the rain, the windy day, the quiet day
My day of course is that of the fisherman.
Provided with line and hook,
O sun give me life
And to my wife, my children, my parents.

—PRAYER OF THANKSGIVING
SAID BY HAWAIIAN FISHERMEN
AFTER CATCHING A FISH

May my body
Be a prayerstick
For the world.

—JOAN HALIFAX

Think of all the years passed by in which you said
to yourself "I'll do it tomorrow,"
and how the gods have again and again granted
you periods of grace
of which you have not availed yourself.
It is time to realize that you are a member
of the Universe,
that you are born of Nature itself,
and to know that a limit has been set to your time.
Use every moment wisely, to perceive
your inner refulgence,
or 'twill be gone and nevermore within your reach.

—MARCUS AURELIUS, TRANSLATED
BY JONATHAN STARI BOW TO THE
ONE WHO HAS NO COLOR,

I bow to the One who has no beginning.
I bow to the One who is without fault,
I bow to the One who is incomprehensible.

I bow to the One who has no treasure,
I bow to the One who is indestructible.
I bow to the Bountiful.
I bow to the Unlimited.

—Sacred song of the Sikhs

Perhaps each of us have a starved place, and each of us knows deep down what we need to fill that place. To find the courage to trust and honor the search, to follow the voice that tells us what we need to do, even when it doesn't seem to make sense, is a worthy pursuit.

—Sue Bender

May the Wind breathe healing upon us,
prolong our life-span,
and fill our hearts with comfort!

You are our father, O Wind,
our friend and our brother.
Give us life that we may live.

From that immortal treasure, O Lord,
which is hidden in your abode,
impart to us that we may live.

—THE VEDAS, TRANSLATED BY
RAIMUNDO PANNIKER

Oh, for the wonder
that bubbles into my soul.

—D. H. LAWRENCE

To all that is brief and fragile
superficial, unstable,
To all that lacks foundation
argument or principles;
To all that is light,
fleeting, changing, finite
To smoke spirals,
wand roses,
To sea foam
and mists of oblivion...
To all that is light in weight
for itinerants
on this transient earth
Somber, raving
with transitory words
and vaporous bubbly wines
I toast
in breakable glasses.

—Maria Eugenia Baz Ferreira

The flute of interior time is played
  whether we hear it or not,
What we mean by "love" is its sound coming in.
When love hits the farthest edge of excess,
  it reaches a wisdom.
And the fragrance of that knowledge!
It penetrates our thick bodies,
it goes through walls—
Its network of notes has a structure as if a million
  suns were arranged inside.
This tune has truth in it.
Where else have you heard a sound like this?

—Kabir, translated by Robert Bly

Love courses through everything,
No, Love is everything.
How can you say, there is no love,
  when nothing but Love exists?
All that you see has appeared because of Love.
  All shines from Love,
  All pulses with Love,
  All flows from Love-
No, once again all is Love!

—Fakhruddin Araqi,
translated by Jonathan Star

May the God of justice and mercy unite us in compassionate solidarity with all those in need, that our lives may be just and merciful, and a source of Her blessing to many.

—Marchiene Vroon Rienstra

When the green woods laugh with the voice of joy,
And the dimpling stream runs laughing by;
When the air does laugh with our merry wit,
And the green hill laughs with the noise of it;

When the meadows laugh with lively green,
And the grasshopper laughs in the merry scene,
When Mary and Susan and Emily
With their sweet round mouths sing "Ha, Ha, He!"

When the painted birds laugh in the shade,
Where our table with cherries and nuts is spread,
Come live & be merry, and join with me,
To sing the sweet chorus of "Ha, Ha, He!"

—William Butler Yeats,
"Laughing Song"

As you eat, know that you are feeding more than just a body. You are feeding the soul's longing for life, its timeless desire to learn the lessons of earthly existence—love and hate, pleasure and pain, fear and faith, illusion and truth—through the vehicle of food. Ultimately, the most important aspect of nutrition is not what to eat but how our relationship to food can teach us who we are and how we can sustain ourselves at the deepest level of being.

—MARC DAVID

Peace be to me
Peace be to my brothers and sisters
who are one with me.
Let all the world be blessed with peace through us.

—ADAPTED FROM *A COURSE IN MIRACLES*

Come, for today is for us a day of festival; henceforward joy and pleasure are on the increase.

Clap hands, say, "Today is all happiness"; from the beginning it was manifestly a fine day.

Who is there in this world like our Friend? Who has seen such a festival in a hundred cycles?

Earth and heaven are filled with sugar; in every direction sugarcane has sprouted.

The roar of that pearl-scattering sea has arrived; the world is full of waves, and the sea is invisible.

—RUMI, TRANSLATED BY A. J. ARBERRY

May we all, in the words of Thomas Berry, "learn to live graciously together on this unique, beautiful, blue planet."

May everyone be happy and safe, and may their hearts be filled with joy.

May all living beings live in Security and in
Peace—beings who are frail or strong, tall or short,
big or small, visible or not visible, near or far away,
already born or yet to be born.
May all of them dwell in perfect tranquility.

Let no one do harm to anyone. Let no one put the life of anyone in danger. Let no one, out of anger or ill will, wish anyone any harm.

—Metta Sutta (Suttanipata),
translated by Thich Nhat Hahn

The God who is in fire, who is in water, who has entered into the whole world, who is in plants, who is in trees—to that God be adoration!

—The Upanishads

I will not die an unlived life.
I will not live in fear
of falling or catching fire.
I choose to inhabit my days,
to allow my living to open me,
to make me less afraid,
more accessible,
to loosen my heart
until it becomes a wing,
a torch, a promise.
I choose to risk my significance;
to live so that which came to me as seed
goes to the next as blossom
and that which came to me as blossom,
goes on as fruit.

—Dawna Markova

Give us grace, O God, to dare to do the deed which we well know cries to be done. Let us not hesitate because of ease, or the words of [people]'s mouths, or our own lives. Mighty causes are calling us—the freeing of women, the training of children, the putting down of hate and murder and poverty—all these and more. But they call with voices that mean work and sacrifice and death. [May we find a way to meet the task.]

—W. E. B. Du Bois

From the cowardice that shrinks from new truth,
From the laziness that is content with half-truths,
From the arrogance that thinks it knows all truth,
O God of Truth, deliver us.

—An ancient scholar

To forgive our brother is to forgive
Ourselves—
We abandon our revenge;
Our lives have seen suffering enough.
We are tired and worn out with
Ourselves—

If I take revenge, it will be the cause;
The effect will follow me into my next life.
Look into the mirror; see the compassion
  in your heart.
Avoid all resentment and hatred for Mankind.

—Le Ly Hayslip

To the good I am good;
to the non-good I am also good,
for Life is goodness.
To the faithful I am faithful;
to the unfaithful I am also faithful,
for Life is faithfulness....
the person of calling accepts them all as his or
her children.

—TAO TE CHING

Holding hands in a ring
I vow with all beings
to ease the pain in the ring
of breath around the world.
When the table is spread for the meal
I vow with all beings
to accept each dish as an offering
that honors my ancient path.

—ROBERT AITKEN

How happy are the poor in spirit;
theirs is the kingdom of heaven.
Happy the gentle:
they shall have the earth for their heritage.

Happy those who mourn:
they shall be comforted.
Happy those who hunger and thirst
  for what is right:
they shall be satisfied.
Happy the merciful:
they shall have mercy shown them.
Happy the pure in heart:
they shall see God.
Happy the peacemakers:
they shall be called children of God.
Happy those who are persecuted
  in the cause of right:
theirs is the kingdom of heaven.

—MATTHEW 5:3-10

It is written in Mahayana Buddhism that "the way is not one of turning away from the world, but of overcoming it through growing toward knowledge, through active love toward one's fellow beings, through inner participation in the joys and sufferings of others and equanimity with regard to one's own weal and woe." May we strive more and more to turn toward life, particularly toward that which we would rather turn away from.

I have arrived.
I am home.
In the here.
In the now.
I am solid.
I am free.
In the ultimate I dwell.

—Thich Nhat Hanh

Tonight we give thanks for the great gift of friendship and in particular for my dear friend, [name]. Thank you for the circumstances that brought us together and have bound us into the sacred bundle of life. Thank you also for the gifts of our friendship: for knowledge that comforts, for words that encourage, for insight that blesses, for all the experiences shared, for the sweet bliss of deeply knowing each other in so many ways; for history and a hope of the future, for conversation and laughter, for silence, for bearing each other's witness truly, for holding each other safe in our hearts with great love and tenderness.

—Daphne Rose Kingma

My heart leaps up when I behold
A rainbow in the sky:
So was it when my life began;
So is it now I am a man;
So be it when I shall grow old,
Or let me die!
The Child is father of the Man;
And I could wish my days to be
Bound each to each by natural piety.

—WILLIAM WORDSWORTH,
"LAUGHING SONG"

Even if heaven and earth turn upside down, it does not mean that they are not at rest, and even if floods overflow heaven, it does not mean that they are in motion.

—SENG-CHAO, "TREATISES"

We give thanks for the Sun even when
behind clouds it hides.
We give thanks for the Wind
though it bend the birches low.
We give thanks for Rain gentle or torrential.
We give thanks for the Earth.
For its Beauty and Glory and Power we
give thanks.
Give us Grace to be good stewards of this
our Inheritance.

—Annabelle Woodard

In the twilight rain
These brilliant-hued hibiscus—
A lovely sunset.

—Basho

Beloved, gaze in thine own heart,
The holy tree is growing there;
From joy the holy branches start,
And all the trembling flowers they bear.
The changing colours of its fruit
Have dowered the stars with merry light;
The surety of its hidden root
Has planted quiet in the night;
The shaking of its leafy head
Has given the waves their melody,
And made my lips and music wed,
Murmuring a wizard song for thee.
There, through bewildered branches, go
Winged Loves borne on in gentle strife,
Tossing and tossing to and fro
The flaming circle of our life.
When looking on their shaken hair,
And dreaming how they dance and dart,
Thine eyes grow full of tender care:
Beloved, gaze in thine own heart.

—William Butler Yeats,
"The Two Trees"

Oh God, whose vast light devours all differences and in whose majesty all prejudices tremble, we pray for an opening of our hearts to all our gay brothers and sisters. We ask you to break down the walls that divide us, that keep us estranged.

Give us compassion for the sufferings they have suffered, violations of the spirit through prejudice, discrimination, and judgment, a plague of illness and death; and may we honor them for the bountiful gifts they have brought us, gifts that expand and nourish our spirits.

We acknowledge the burden they have carried in being the living embodiment of the blending of the male and female energies, and give thanks for their living out of the message that human essence is not of the body but of the spirit, not of gender but of consciousness, not of prejudice but of great love.

—Daphne Rose Kingma

There is in all things an inexhaustible sweetness and purity, a silence that is a fount of action and joy. It rises up in wordless gentleness and flows out to me from the unseen roots of all created being, welcoming me tenderly, saluting me with indescribable humility.

—Thomas Merton

Earth brings us into life
and nourishes us.
Earth takes us back again.
Birth and death are present in every moment.

—Thich Nhat Hanh

There is no shortage of good days. It is good lives that are hard to come by. A life of good days lived in the senses is not enough. The life of sensation is the life of greed; it requires more and more. The life of the spirit requires less and less; time is ample and its passage sweet.

—Annie Dillard

The Chinese sage Lao Tzu once said, "He or she who knows that enough is enough will always have enough." May we learn to be grateful for whatever we have so that it may be enough.

All the cattle are resting in the fields,
The trees and the plants are growing,
The birds flutter above the marshes,
Their wings uplifted in adoration,
And all the sheep are dancing,
All winged things are flying,
They live when you have shone on them.

—Ancient Egyptian poem to the sun

I am aware that I owe so much to my parents,
teacher, friends, and all beings.
I vow to be worthy of their trust,
to practice wholeheartedly,
so that Understanding and Compassion will flower,
and I can help living beings be free from their
suffering.

—Thich Nhat Hanh

There is nothing I can give you
which you do have not;
But there is much, very much, that
while I cannot give it, you can take.

No heaven can come to us unless our hearts
find rest in today. Take heaven!
No peace lies in the future which is not hidden
in this present instant. Take peace!

The gloom of the world is but a shadow.
Behind it, yet within reach, is joy.
There is a radiance and glory in the
darkness, could
we but see,
and to see, we have only to look. I beseech you
to look.

—Fra Giovanni, A.D. 1513

Late have I loved you, O Beauty so ancient and so new; late have I loved you! For behold you were within me, and I outside; and I sought you outside and in my unloveliness fell upon those things that you have made. You were with me and I was not with you. I was kept from you by those things, yet had they not been in you, they would not have been at all. You called and cried to me and broke open my deafness; you sent your shafts of light to shine on me and chase away my blindness; you breathed your fragrant breath on me, and I took a breath and now pant for you; I tasted you, and now I hunger and thirst for you; you touched me and I have burned for your peace.

—Saint Augustine

Holy One of Blessing,
Your Presence fills creation.

—Rabbi Lawrence S. Kushner

On this day, we pray for tender compassion on all the little ones, whose new souls, so fresh from the light, shine in our midst with a darling adorable brightness.

May we honor them deeply, learn from them truly, respecting the deep wisdom they carry. Make us wise in our nurturing of them, generous in our loving, unending in our compassion, expansive with our wisdom, kind with our intelligence, and graceful with our hearts. Let us give to them and receive from them, and let it be known among us that they are neither our projects nor our possessions, but messengers of light, illuminations of love.

—DAPHNE ROSE KINGMA

I sing for the animals,
Out of the earth I sing for them.
A Horse nation
I sing for them.
Out of the earth
I sing for them,
The animals
I sing for them.

—Teton Sioux

[First person]: Praised are You,
[Second person]: Lord our God, Ruler of the Universe, He
[Third person]: who causes bread to emerge from the earth.

—From Blessings: Invoking the Life Moment

Glory be to God for dappled things—
For skies of couple-color as a brinded cow;
For rose-moles all in stipple
upon trout that swim;
Fresh-firecoal chestnut-falls; finches' wings;
Landscape plotted and pieced—fold, fallow,
and plough;
And all trades, their gear and tackle
and trim.

All things counter, original, spare, strange;
Whatever is fickle, freckled
(who knows how?)
With swift, slow; sweet, sour; adazzle, dim;
He fathers—forth whose beauty is past change:
Praise him

—GERARD MANLEY HOPKINS

Praised be you, my Lord, through our Sister Mother Earth, who sustains us, governs us, and who produces varied fruits with colored flowers and herbs.

Praised be you, my Lord, through Brother Wind and through the air, cloudy and serene, and every kind of weather.

Praised be you, my Lord, through Sister Moon and the stars in heaven; you formed them clear and precious and beautiful.

Praised be you, my Lord, through Brother Fire, through whom you light the night and he is beautiful and playful and robust and strong.

Praised be you, my Lord, with all your creatures, especially Sir Brother Sun, who is the day and through whom you give us light. And he is beautiful and radiant with great splendors and bears likeness of You, Most High One.

—Saint Francis of Assisi

There is no form without the gift of the Mother and the Father. From Father Sky comes your consciousness and Mother Earth is your very bones. To sense the balance of the Mother/Father, Father/Mother within one's own being, one's own nature, is a way to renew the Earth, to renew our hearts, to renew the vision.

—Dhyani Ywahoo

Be tough in the way a blade of grass is: rooted, willing to lean, and at peace with what is around it.

—Natalie Goldberg

What is well planted cannot be uprooted . . .
Cultivate Virtue in your own person,
And it becomes a genuine part of you.
Cultivate it in the family,
And it will abide.
Cultivate it in the community,
And it will live and grow.
Cultivate it in the state,
And it will flourish abundantly.
Cultivate it in the world,
And it will become universal.

—Tao Te Ching

Silence hovers over all the mountain peaks. The world is aflame with grandeur. Each flower is an outpouring of love. Each being speaks for itself. Man alone can speak of all beings. Human living alone enacts the mystery as a drama.

—Abraham Joshua Heschel

I do not ask to walk smooth paths
nor bear an easy load.
I pray for strength and fortitude
to climb the rock strewn road.

Give me such courage and I can scale
the headiest peaks alone,
And transform every stumbling block
into a stepping stone.

—Gail Brook Burket

Let there be everywhere our voices, our eyes, our thoughts, our love, our actions, breathing hope and victory.

—Sonia Sanchez

Earth mother, star mother,
You who are called by
  a thousand names,
May all remember
  we are cells in your body
  and dance together.
You are the grain
  and the loaf
That sustains us each day.
And as you are patient
  with our struggles to learn
So shall we be patient
  with ourselves and each other.
We are radiant light
  and sacred dark
—the balance—
You are the embrace that heartens
And the freedom beyond fear.
Within you we are born
  we grow, live, and die—
You bring us around the circle
  to rebirth,
Within us you dance
Forever.

—Starhawk, "The Spiral Dance"

Be patient with everyone, but above all with yourself... do not be disheartened by your imperfections, but always rise up with fresh courage. How are we to be patient in dealing with our neighbor's faults if we are impatient in dealing with our own? They who are fretted by their own failings will not correct them. All profitable correction comes from a calm and peaceful mind.

—Saint Francis de Sales

From time flow forth created things
From time, too, they advance in growth.
Likewise in time they disappear.
Time is a form and formless, too.

—The Upanishads

To be joyful in the universe is a brave and reckless act. The courage for joy springs not from the certainty of human experience, but the surprise. Our astonishment at being loved, our bold willingness to love in return—these wonders promise the possibility of joyfulness, no matter how often and how harshly love seems to be lost.

Therefore, despite the world's sorrows, we give thanks for our loves, for our joys and for the continued courage to be happily surprised.

—Molly Fumia

We may wonder whom can I love and serve? Where is the face of God to whom I can pray? The answer is simple. That naked one. That lonely one. That unwanted one is my brother and my sister. If we have no peace, it is because we have forgotten that we belong to each other.

—Mother Teresa

Each day of human life contains joy and anger, pain and pleasure, darkness and light, growth and decay. Each moment is etched with nature's great design—do not try to deny or oppose the cosmic order of things. Always try to be in communion with heaven and earth; then the world will appear in its true light.

—Morihei Ueshiba

One perfect moon
  and the uncountable
  stars
drowned in a green sky

—Shiki

The Universe is immense and gorgeous and magnificent. I salute it. Every speck, every little fly on the window salutes the Universe. Every leaf has meaning. I think the Universe is expanding—it is experiencing and accomplishing. And we have the opportunity to add to its glow. Everybody can love, in the place where they are. In the physical body in which [we] are. In the life in which [we] are involved. We can all add our share of love without leaving the room.

—Helen Nearing

No one can give
what he or she hasn't received.
So as we are blessed, we
bless the world,
giving thanks for every living thing
for otherwise we offer thanks for nothing.

—Adapted from A Course in Miracles

To compose our character is our duty, not to compose books.... Our great and glorious masterpiece is to live appropriately. All other things, to rule, to lay up treasure, to build, are at most but little appendices and props.... For my part, then, I love life and cultivate it, such as it has pleased God to bestow it upon us.... I accept heartily and gratefully what Nature has done for me, and I am pleased with myself and proud of myself for it. We do wrong to that great and omnipotent Giver by refusing his gift, nullifying and disfiguring it. Being all good, he has made all things good.

—Montaigne

Thank you for the reflection of Your Smile in all we see.

—Kenneth Kurtz

I honor the God and the Goddess,
The eternal parents of the universe...

Without the God
  there is no Goddess,
And without the Goddess
  there is no God...

The life of one
  is the life of the other,
And not even a blade of grass can grow
  without the both of them.

—Jnaneshwar, translated by Jonathan Star

A perception, sudden as blinking,
that subject and object are one,
will lead to a deeply mysterious
  wordless understanding;
and by this understanding you will awaken
  to the truth.

—Hung Po

May we live our lives beyond separation, knowing that nations and cultures are made up of individuals. May I be as one who rethinks my life, my actions, and aligns to the glory we are all capable of. May I follow where I am spiritually guided, and embrace what is new that is of love. May love flow through me and lend my individual life and light toward a better world.

—Jacqueline T. Snyder (Eagle Speaks Woman), Founder of Sacred Life Association

---

Thank you for the wind and rain
and sun and pleasant weather,
thank you for this our food
and that we are together.

—Mennonite blessing

Would that you could live on the fragrance of the earth, and like an air plant be sustained by the light.

But since you must kill to eat, and rob the newly born of its mother's milk to quench your thirst, let it then be an act of worship.

And let your board stand an altar on which the pure and the innocent of forest and plain are sacrificed for that which is purer and still more innocent in man.

When you kill a beast say to him in your heart,

"By the same power that slays you, I too am slain; and I too shall be consumed.

For the law that delivered you into my hand shall deliver me into a mightier hand.

Your blood and my blood is naught but the sap that feeds the tree of heaven."

And when you crush an apple with your teeth, say to it in your heart,

"Your seeds shall live in my body,

And the buds of your tomorrow shall blossom in my heart,

And your fragrance shall be my breath,

And together we shall rejoice through all the seasons."

—Kahlil Gibran

Christianity has been reproached for trying to deceive people about the reality of earthly suffering by comfort- ing them with the prospect of heavenly blessedness awaiting them. Jesus was not thinking of vague future bliss. For he does not say: Blessed eventually will be those who now suffer. Rather he promises: Blessed are you now, right this minute, while you are suffering.

—ALBERT SCHWEITZER

Give us grateful hearts, our Mother, for all thy mercies, and make us mindful of the needs of others.

Amen.

—ADAPTED FROM *THE BOOK OF COMMON PRAYER*

Ho! Great One!
I thank you for my life.

Ho! Spirits of the water
I thank you for satisfying my thirst.
I thank you for cleansing me physically,
Emotionally and spiritually.
I thank you, for when I drink,
My emotions are calmed.

Ho! Spirits of the wind
I thank you for cooling me
When I am hot.
I thank you for singing in my ears
When my spirit needs music.
I thank you for whispering messages.

Ho! Spirits of the fire
I thank you for keeping me
Warm when it is cold.
I thank you for burning the evil
And taking it back to the light.

Ho! Spirits of the Earth
I thank you for protecting
Our sweet mother earth.
I thank you for giving me the foods
I need for nourishment.

Ho! Great One!
I thank you for being your child.
Ho! Yes!!
I thank you!

—LILIANA GAMBARTE

Earth, arise in each of us.

—ANONYMOUS

1

Have you not wounded yourself
And battered those you love
By sudden motions of evil,
Black rage in the blood
When the soul, premier danseur,
Springs toward a murderous fall?
The furies possess you.

2

Have you not surprised yourself
Sometimes by sudden motions
Or intimations of goodness,
When the soul, premier danseur,
Perfectly poised,
Could shower blessings
With a graceful turn on the head?
The angels are there.

3

The angels, the furies
Are never far away
While we dance, we dance,
Trying to keep a balance,
To be perfectly human

(Not perfect, never perfect,
Never an end to growth and peril),
Able to bless and forgive
Ourselves.
This is what is asked of us.

4

It is light that matters,
The light of understanding.
Who has ever reached it
Who has not met the furies again and again?
Who has reached it without
Those sudden acts of grace?

—May Sarton, "The Angels and the Furies"

May we become, as Ram Dass has written, "hollow reeds for the healing music of life."

I am the one whose praise echoes on high
I adorn all the earth
I am the breeze that nurtures all things green
I encourage blossoms to flourish with
    ripening fruits.
I am led by the spirit to feed the purest streams.
I am the rain coming from the dew
that causes the grasses to laugh with the joy of life.
I am the yearning for good.

—Hildegard of Bingen

When I walk through thy woods,
may my right foot and my left foot
be harmless to the little creatures
that move in its grasses: as it is said
by the mouth of thy prophet,
They shall not hurt nor destroy
in all my holy mountain.

—Rabbi Moshe Hakotun

Let us not run the world hastily,
Let us not grasp at the rope of wealth impatiently;
What should be treated with mature judgement,
Let us not treat in a fit of temper;
Whenever we arrive at a cool place,
Let us rest sufficiently well;
Let us give prolonged attention to the future,
And then let us give due regard to the consequence
of things,
And that is on account of our sleeping.

—Yoruba odu (recital),
translated by E. B. Idowu

Every particle of the world is a mirror,
In each atom lies the blazing light
    of a thousand suns.
Cleave the heart of a rain-drop,
    a hundred pure oceans will flow forth.
Look closely at a grain of sand,
    the seed of a thousand beings can be seen.
The foot of an ant is larger than an elephant;
In essence, a drop of water
    is no different than the Nile.
In the heart of a barley-corn
    lies the fruit of a hundred harvests;
Within the pulp of a millet seed
    an entire universe can be found.
In the wing of a fly,
    an ocean of wonder;
In the pupil of the eye, an endless heaven.
Though the inner chamber of the heart is small,
    the Lord of both worlds
    gladly makes His home there.

—Mahmud Shabistari,
translated by Jonathan Star

As Jack Kornfield notes, "In the end we can see this either as a world where we all eat and are eaten or as a world where we all have an opportunity to feed one another." Let us rededicate ourselves today to doing all we can to feed one another.

Give me strength to refrain from the unkind silence that is born of hardness of heart; the unkind silence that clouds the serenity of understanding and is the enemy of peace.

Give me strength to be the first to tender the healing word and the renewal of friendship, that the bonds of amity and the flow of charity may be strengthened.

—Cecil Hunt

Blessed are the man and the woman
who have grown beyond their greed
and have put an end to their hatred
and no longer nourish illusions.
But they delight in the way things are
and keep their hearts open, day and night.
They are like trees planted near flowing rivers,
which bear fruit when they are ready.
Their leaves will not fall or wither.
Everything they do will succeed.

—Psalm 1:1, translated
by Stephen Mitchell

It is time to come to your senses. You are to live and to learn to laugh. You are to learn to listen to the cursed radio music of life and to reverence the spirit behind it and to laugh at its distortions. So there you are. More will not be asked of you.

—Herman Hesse

Center of all centers, core of cores,
almond self-enclosed and growing sweet—
all this universe, to the furthest stars
and beyond them, is your flesh, your fruit.

Now you feel how nothing clings to you;
your vast shell reaches into endless space,
and there the rich, thick fluids rise and flow.
Illuminated in your infinite peace,

a billion stars go spinning through the night,
blazing high above your head.
But in you is the presence that
will be, when all the stars are dead.

—Rainer Maria Rilke, "Buddha In Glory," translated by Stephen Mitchell

Always we hope
someone else has the answer.
Some other place will be better,
some other time
it will all turn out.

This is it.
No one else has the answer.
No other place will be better,
and it has already turned out.

At the center of your being you have the answer;
you know who you are and you know
what you want.

There is no need
to run outside
for better seeing.

Nor to peer from a window.

Rather abide at
the center of your being;
for the more you leave it
the less you learn.

Search your heart
and see
the way to do
is to be.

—Lao Tzu, translator unknown

Almighty God, grant us grace fearlessly to contend against evil, and to make no peace with oppression; and, that we may reverently use our freedom, help us to employ it in the maintenance of justice among people and nations.

—Adapted from *The Book of Common Prayer*

Where will you place the "talent" you have been given? We must ask that question afresh each day, each year. Where will you focus the potential for creative action that is yours? Those are the questions before the man and the woman of our time. I think we do not improve on the answer given by Isaiah twenty-five hundred years ago, "Here am I, Lord, send me."

Send me into the village square, send me into schools, send me into the day camps for children, send me into the task of creating beauty, send me into the business world to create more jobs, send me into the political world to struggle for the values I hold dear, send me into the earth as her son, to love her and to cherish her. Send me to help create the "thousand healths and hidden isles" not even yet imagined. Then I will know that I have lived and loved well with this precious gift of life that has been given to me.

—Dwight H. Judy

You often say, "I would give, but only to the
deserving."
The trees in your orchard say not so, nor the
flocks in your pastures.
They give that they may live, for to withhold
is to perish.

—KAHLIL GIBRAN

In the end the love you take
is equal to the love you make.

—JOHN LENNON AND PAUL MCCARTNEY

Index

D

E

F

S

T

Acknowledgments

Bountiful thanks to Karen Bouris for the initial impulse and enduring enthusiasm, Carol Baker for nimble fingers and a willing spirit, Elizabeth von Radics for red-pencil proficiency, Jennifer Brontsema for layout know-how, Emily Miles for expert publicity pushings, Will Glennon for forcing me into Conari Press in the first place, and Michael Levine, Susan Jack, Robin Lysne, and Barb Parmet for pointing me in helpful directions.

I also want to acknowledge the inspiration of Benedictine monk Brother David Steindl-Rast's book, *Gratefulness, The Heart of Prayer* and his audiotape, *The Grateful Heart*. For those who want to delve into the deeper meanings of gratitude, I can't recommend his work highly enough.

Special thanks to the writers who took time out of their hectic lives to contribute blessings specifically for this collection: Angeles Arrien, Diane V. Cirincione, Molly Fumia, Liliana Gambarte, Joan Halifax, Lex Hixon, Gerald G. Jampolsky, M.D., Daphne Rose Kingma, Jack Kornfield, Kenneth R. Kurtz, John Lee, Bernie Siegel, M.D., Jacqueline T. Snyder, Sue Patton Thoele, and Annabelle Woodard.

Copyright Acknowledgments

Thanks for permission to excerpt from the following previously published works:

Mystical Poems of Rumi by A. J. Arberry. Copyright © 1968 by A. J. Arberry. Reprinted by permission of The University of Chicago Press. *Plain and Simple* by Sue Bender. Copyright © 1989 by Sue Bender. Reprinted by permission of the author. *Safe Passage* by Molly Fumia. Copyright © 1992 by Molly Fumia. Reprinted by permission of Conari Press. *The Art of the Possible* by Dawna Markova, Ph.D. Copyright © 1991 by Dawna Markova, Ph.D. Reprinted by permission of Conari Press. *A Garland of Love* by Daphne Rose Kingma. Copyright © 1992 by Daphne Rose Kingma. Reprinted by permission of Conari Press. *Plum Village Chanting Book* by Eglise Bouddhique Unfiee. Copyright © 1991. Reprinted by permission of Parallax Press, Berkeley, CA. *Present Moment Wonderful Moment: Mindfulness Verse for Daily Living* by Thich Nhat Hanh. Copyright © 1990. Reprinted by permission of Parallax Press, Berkeley, CA. *The Dragon Who Never Sleeps: Verses for Zen Buddhist Practice* by Robert Aitken (1992) reprinted by permission of Parallax Press, Berkeley CA. *When Heaven and Earth Changed Places* by Le Ly Hayslip. Copyright © 1989 by Le Ly Hayslip and Charles Jay Wurts. Used by permission of Doubleday, a division of Bantam Doubleday Dell Publishing Group, Inc.. *Hearts on Fire,* edited by Michael Harter, SJ. Copyright © 1993. Used by permission of the Institute of Jesuit Sources, St. Louis, MO. *Workbook for Spiritual Development of All People* by Hua-Ching Ni. Copyright © 1984, 1992. Used by permission of SevenStar Communications, 1314 Second St.,Santa Monica, CA 90401 (310) 576-1901. *The Sacred in the Simple*, copyright © Mary Lou Kownacki, OSB. *Let Us Pray* by Robert French Leavens. Copyright © 1939 by Robert French Leavens. Used by permission of Eucalyptus Press, Oakland, CA. *Secrets of the Heart* by Kahlil Gibran. Copyright © 1975 by

Philosophical Library. Published by arrangement with Carol Publishing Group. A Citadel Press Book. *Manual of Zen Buddhism* by D. T. Suzuki. Reprinted by permission of Grove Atlantic. One stanza from "A Dialogue of Self and Soul" by W. B. Yeats. Reprinted by permission of Macmillian Publishing Company from *The Poems of W.B. Yeats: A New Edition* by Richard J. Finneran. Copyright © 1933 by Macmillian Publishing Company, renewed 1961 by Bertah Georgie Yeats. Reprinted by permission of Macmillian Publishing Company, Inc.. *The Way of Lao Tzu,* translated by Wing-Tsit Chan. Copyright © 1963 by Macmillian College Publishing Company, Inc.. Reprinted by permission of Macmillian Publishing Company, Inc.. *Acts of Faith* by Iyanla Vanzant. Copyright © 1993 by Iyanla Vanzant. All Rights Reserved. Reprinted by permission of Marie Brown Associates. *Tao Te Ching* by Lao Tsu, translated by Gia-Fu Feng and Jane English. Copyright © 1972 by Gia-Fu Feng and Jane English. Reprinted by permission of Alfred A. Knopf, Inc..*Coming Out to God: Prayers for Lesbians and Gay Men, Their Families and Friends* by Chris Glaser. Copyright © 1991 by Chris Glaser. Used by permission of Westminster/John Knox Press. *Collected Poems of May Sarton 1930-1993* by May Sarton. Copyright © 1971, 1972 by May Sarton. Reprinted by permission of W. W. Norton & Company, Inc. *The Kabir Book* by Robert Bly. Copyright © 1971, 1977 by Robert Bly. Reprinted by permission of Beacon Press. *Two Suns Rising* by Jonathan Star. Translation copyright © 1991 by Jonathan Star. Used by permission of Bantam Books, a division of Bantam Doubleday Dell Publishing Group, Inc.. *Swallows Nest: A Feminine Reading of the Psalms* by Marchine Vroon Rienstra. Copyright © 1992. Used by permission of Wm. B. Eerdmans Publishing Co. *The Measure of Our Success* by Marian Wright Edelman. Copyright © 1992 by Marian Wright Edelman. Reprinted by permission of Beacon Press. *Wrestling the Light: Ache and Awe in the Human-Divine Struggle* by Ted Loder. Copyright © 1991 by LuraMedia. Reprinted by permission of LuraMedia, Inc., San Diego, CA. *Na Pule Kahiko* by June Gutmanis. Copyright © 1984 by June Gutmanis. Reprinted by permission of Editions, Limited,

P.O. Box 10236, Honolulu, HI 96816. 11 lines and 10 lines from *The Enlightened Heart* by Stephen Mitchell. Copyright by Stephen Mitchell. Reprinted by permission of HarperCollins Publishers, Inc.. 6 lines and 28 lines from *Seasons of Your Heart: Prayers and Reflections* by Macrina Wiederkehr. Copyright © 1991 by Macrina Wiederkehr. Reprinted by permission of HarperCollins Publishers, Inc.. "Great Man Going" by Stephen W. Hyde. Reprinted by permission of the author. "So Much Happiness" by Naomi Shihab Nye from *Hugging the Jukebox*. Reprinted by permission of the author. *Prayers of the Social Awakening* by Walter Rauschenbusch Withorn. Copyright by Pilgrim Press, Cleveland, OH. Reprinted by permission. 24 lines from *The Star Dance* by Starhawk. Copyright © 1979 by Miriam Simos. Reprinted by permission of HarperCollins Publishers, Inc.. Selection from *Nature Meditations* by Hazrat Inayat Khan. Reprinted by permission of the Sufi Order. "The End" by John Lennon and Paul McCartney. Copyright © 1969 Northern Songs Ltd. All Rights Controlled by EMI Blackwood Music Inc., under license from ATV Music Corp. (Maclen Music). All Rights Reserved. International Copyright secured. Used by permission. Selections from pp. 19 and 23 of *The Mood of Christmas* and page 123 of *Meditations of the Heart* (originally, from *The Mood of Christmas*) by Howard Thurman. Reprinted by permission of Anne Thurman, Director of the Howard Thurman Educational Trust Fund. The lines from "i thank You God for most this amazing" from *Complete Poems, 1904–1962*, by E. E. Cummings, edited by George J. Firmage, are reprinted by permission of Liveright Publishing Corporation. Copyright © 1950, 1978, 1991 by the Trustees for the E. E. Cummings Trust.

An exhaustive effort has been made to clear all reprint permissions for this book. This process has been complicated; if any required acknowledgments have been omitted, it is unintentional. If notified, the publishers will be pleased to rectify any omission in future editions.

About the Editor

Best-selling author M. J. Ryan is the former CEO and co-founder of Conari Press in Berkeley, California. One of the creators of the bestselling *Random Acts of Kindness*™ series (over one million copies in print), she is the author of *Attitudes of Gratitude, The Giving Heart, 365 Health and Happiness Boosters,* and, under the nom de plume Susannah Seton, the *Simple Pleasures* series. She is also the editor of the award-winning book *The Fabric of the Future*.

She is currently a consultant with Professional Thinking Partners, where she specializes in coaching senior-level executives, small business owners, entrepreneurs, and other professionals on issues of life purpose, leadership development, and collaborative thinking. She is also one of the facilitators of TimeOut, a five-day bimonthly retreat on personal renewal for corporate executives and other professionals at Robert Redford's resort in Sundance, Utah. A popular speaker and workshop leader on what she is calling "the modern virtues"—simplicity, gratitude, generosity, and kindness—her work has appeared in numerous newspapers and magazines, including USA Today, Family Circle, Yoga Journal, and Body and Soul.

Visit her Web site at www.maryjaneryan.com.

To Our Readers

Mango Publishing, established in 2014, publishes an eclectic list of books by diverse authors—both new and established voices—on topics ranging from business, personal growth, women's empowerment, LGBTQ studies, health, and spirituality to history, popular culture, time management, decluttering, lifestyle, mental wellness, aging, and sustainable living. We were recently named 2019 and 2020's #1 fastest growing independent publisher by *Publishers Weekly*. Our success is driven by our main goal, which is to publish high quality books that will entertain readers as well as make a positive difference in their lives.

Our readers are our most important resource; we value your input, suggestions, and ideas. We'd love to hear from you—after all, we are publishing books for you!

Please stay in touch with us and follow us at:

Facebook: Mango Publishing
Twitter: @MangoPublishing
Instagram: @MangoPublishing
LinkedIn: Mango Publishing
Pinterest: Mango Publishing
Newsletter: mangopublishinggroup.com/newsletter

Join us on Mango's journey to reinvent publishing, one book at a time.